THE
Courage
and Character *of*
THEODORE
ROOSEVELT

Also by George Grant

Carry a Big Stick
The Uncommon Heroism of Theodore Roosevelt

Grand Illusions
The Legacy of Planned Parenthood

The Importance of the Electoral College

The Micah Mandate
Balancing the Christian Life

The Patriot's Handbook
A Citizenship Primer for a New Generation of Americans

The Pocket Patriot
An Introduction to the Principles of Freedom

with Gregory Wilbur
The Christian Almanac
*A Dictionary of Days Celebrating History's
Most Significant People and Events*

THE
Courage
and Character of
THEODORE ROOSEVELT

A HERO AMONG LEADERS

GEORGE GRANT

CUMBERLAND HOUSE

NASHVILLE, TENNESSEE

THE COURAGE AND CHARACTER OF THEODORE ROOSEVELT
PUBLISHED BY CUMBERLAND HOUSE PUBLISHING, INC.
431 Harding Industrial Drive
Nashville, Tennessee 37211

Copyright © 1996, 2005 by George Grant

All Scripture quotations, unless otherwise noted, are taken from the *King James Version*. Scripture quotations marked (ASV) are taken from the *American Standard Version* (1901).

Previously published as a volume in the Leaders in Action series as *Carry a Big Stick: The Uncommon Heroism of Theodore Roosevelt*.

Cover design by Gore Studio, Nashville, Tennessee

Library of Congress Cataloging-in-Publication Data

Grant, George, 1954–
    The courage and character of Theodore Roosevelt : a hero among leaders / George Grant.
        p.   cm.
    Rev. ed. of: Carry a big stick. 1st Cumberland House ed. 1996.
    ISBN 1-58182-439-4 (pbk. : alk. paper)
    1. Roosevelt, Theodore, 1858–1919. 2. Presidents—United States—Biography.
3. Political Leadership—United States—Case studies. I. Grant, George, 1954– Carry a big stick. II. Title.
E757.G715 2005
973.91'1'092—dc22

ISBN: 978-1-58182-439-1
ISBN: 978-1-68442-182-4

2004030469

To my grandson:
Joel David Grant II

and to my students:
FCS and Gileskirk

A new generation of leaders

Contents

THE CHARACTER OF THEODORE ROOSEVELT

THE LEGACY OF THEODORE ROOSEVELT

Acknowledgments

If I preach to you anything which I do not strive, with whatever haltings and shortcomings, myself to realize, then I am unworthy your paying heed to me.[1]

BIOGRAPHICAL LABORS are inevitably the fruit of child hood ideals," stated Scottish historian John Buchan. "The seeds sown in early years bear a harvest of intellectual wonderment in latter years."[2]

Indeed, my father first introduced me to the life and exploits of Theodore Roosevelt. When I was a young boy he gave me a small chapbook that became one of my most prized possessions. It still is. Later he encouraged my fascination with this great man by taking me to sites associated with his varied career. The seeds my father sowed so many years ago continue to bear much fruit in my life—and for that I will always be grateful.

The good people at both Highland Books and Cumberland House also heartily encouraged me in pursuing my interests in Roosevelt. Phil Hibbard, Will Wallace, Heather Armstrong, Ron Pitkin, and Dean Andreola have been far more patient and generous than I could have ever asked.

In addition, a number of other friends and fellow laborers have urged me to press ahead with this book and the leadership series of which it was a part—and, at the same time, have helped to support the work of the King's Meadow Study Center so that I could. I can't imagine doing without the gracious encouragement of Ray Ware, Stephen Mansfield, Mike Smith, Scott Roley, Jim and Gwen Smith, Scotty and Darlene Smith, Ian and Ann Sears, Darrow and Marilyn Miller, and Steve and Marijean Green all have been selfless supporters from the beginning. Jim and Anne Kennedy, Gene and Susan Hunt, Tom and Yo Clark, and David and Diane Vaughan guided me through many a rocky shoal with their wise counsel and friendship.

Mike Hyatt first suggested that I consider turning my writing proclivities toward biographies. Jan Dennis, David Dunham, and Robert Wolgemuth gave me my first opportunities to try my hand at this rather demanding discipline. And Otto Scott pointed the way for me by providing the appropriate models from which to learn.

The soundtrack for this project was provided by Michael Card, Anuna, Deanta, and HEM; the midnight musings were provided by Richard Weaver, Colin Thubron, Hilaire Belloc, and G. K. Chesterton.

To all these, I offer my sincerest thanks.

I suppose I probably ought to mention the Nine Muses, the Three Graces, and the Merry Band of Joyeuse Garde as well, but the fact is my greatest and best inspiration comes from my family. Karen is without a doubt a "help meet" for me. And Joel, Joanna, and Jesse are the pride of my life. Their love and unwavering faithfulness remain my greatest hope and richest resource. To them I owe my all in all.

Introduction

*Every great nation owes to the men whose lives have
formed part of its greatness not merely the material effect
of what they did, not merely the laws they placed upon
the statute books or the victories they won over armed
foes, but also the immense but indefinable moral
influence produced by their deeds and words themselves
upon the national character.*[3]

BY ANY measure Theodore Roosevelt was a remarkable man. Before
his fiftieth birthday he had served as a New York state legislator, the
undersecretary of the navy, police commissioner for the city of New
York, U.S. civil service commissioner, the governor of the state of
New York, the vice president under William McKinley, a colonel in
the U.S. Army, and two terms as the president of the United States.

In addition, he had run a cattle ranch in the Dakota Territory,
served as a reporter and editor for several journals, newspapers, and
magazines, and conducted scientific expeditions on four continents.
He read at least five books every week of his life and wrote nearly
fifty on an astonishing array of subjects—from history and biography
to natural science and social criticism.

He enjoyed hunting, boxing, and wrestling. He was an amateur
taxidermist, botanist, ornithologist, and astronomer. He was a

devoted family man who lovingly raised six children. And he enjoyed a lifelong romance with his wife.

During his long and varied career, he was hailed by supporters and rivals alike as the greatest man of the age—perhaps one of the greatest of all ages.[4] According to Thomas Reed, Speaker of the House of Representatives, he was a "new-world Bismarck and Cromwell combined."[5] President Grover Cleveland described him as "one of the ablest men yet produced in human history."[6] Senator Henry Cabot Lodge asserted, "Since Caesar, perhaps no one has attained among crowded duties and great responsibilities, such high proficiency in so many separate fields of activity."[7] After an evening in his company, the epic poet Rudyard Kipling wrote, "I curled up on the seat opposite and listened and wondered until the universe seemed to be spinning round—and Roosevelt was the spinner."[8] Great Britain's Lord Charnwood exclaimed, "No statesman for centuries has had his width of intellectual range; to be sure no intellectual has so touched the world with action."[9] Even his lifelong political opponent, William Jennings Bryan, was bedazzled by his prowess. "Search the annals of history if you will," he said. "Never will you find a man more remarkable in every way than he."[10]

The times that this remarkable man lived in were themselves quite remarkable—the sunset of one century and the dawning of another. The United States had grown from sixteen states in 1800 to forty-five in 1900, from nine hundred thousand square miles to almost four million, and from a population of five million to seventy-six million. That century had produced steamships, railroads, streetcars, bicycles, roller skates, the air brake, the torpedo, telephones, telegraphs, transatlantic cables, harvesting machines, threshers, cotton gins, cooking ranges, sewing machines, phonographs, typewriters, electric lights, illuminating gas, photographs, x-rays, motion pictures, and cottonseed oil. According to journalist Edward Byrn, the comparison of the start of the century with the end of the century was "like the juxtaposition of a distant star with the noonday sun."[11] And popular historian M. J. de Forest Shelton exclaimed that there was "more difference between Napoleon's day and ours than between Napoleon's and Julius Caesar's. One century against eighteen."[12] English intellectual Frederic Harrison agreed: "Take it all in all, the merely material, physical, mechanical change in human life in the hundred years, from the days of Watt and Arkwright to our own, is greater than occurred in the thousand years that preceded, perhaps even the two thousand or twenty thousand years."[13]

Despite bitter labor agitation, anarchist strikes, communist insurgencies, and the emergence of terrorism as a political weapon; despite attempts on the lives of the Prince of Wales, the German emperor, and the shah of Persia; despite successful assassinations of King Umberto of Italy and President McKinley; despite the uproar of the Dreyfus affair in France and the Robida scandal in Austria; despite the imminent passing of the Old World Order with its accompanying specter; despite everything, a robust optimism pervaded the thinking of most Westerners. Their advances, after all, had been stunning. So, for the most part, they shared the opinion of the New York World in its prediction that the new century would "meet and overcome all perils and prove to be the best that this steadily improving planet has ever seen."[14]

Theodore Roosevelt had a saner view—a more realistic view—of his time. It was a view balanced by a Christian understanding of mankind—made in the very image of God, but at the same time, fallen. Perhaps that is the most remarkable thing about this remarkable man: he actually understood his remarkable times and what remarkable things had to be done in order to sustain them.

Roosevelt saw all too clearly the dark dangers that loomed as the Western world marched so boldly, so confidently, into the twentieth century. That is why he devoted himself to remedying as many dangers as possible throughout his life. His political crusades and social reforms focused on the poor working man, on the struggling immigrant, on the miserable tenement dweller, on the helpless widow and orphan, on the despised victims of racial or ethnic prejudice, and on the pioneering homesteader.

By the taint of today's rigidly ideological standards, he was a bundle of contradictions and cross-purposes: sometimes he coursed to the left, sometimes to the right; sometimes he was a champion of mugwumps and progressives, sometimes of standpats and monopolists; sometimes he was the guardian of labor, sometimes of capital; sometimes he was the voice of hawkish expansionism, sometimes of dovish nationalism. But to Roosevelt, there was never a contradiction in his seemingly conflicting positions. In fact, he was unswayed—and even repelled—by the traditional categories of partisanism. Instead, he tenaciously pursued the path of truth and justice—wherever. To this day he is a sort of universal hero: captive to no single interest, no single party, and no single movement. It was almost as if he were above the petty fray.

Perhaps, then, the reason he continues to stand out as one of the greatest leaders in the history of the United States is this: he was willing to use his dynamic accomplishments and prescient gifts for the good of all those around him and of all those who would come after him—regardless of the possible political or career consequences. That kind of moral and intellectual heroism is highly uncommon in this day of standardless pragmatism and cunning latitudinarianism.

This book, the second in a series of biographical profiles of leaders in action, is designed to give readers a glimpse of the character that made possible Theodore Roosevelt's uncommon independence of heart, mind, and spirit—indeed, his uncommon heroism. It is certainly not intended to be a comprehensive look at his life and work—there are many fine biographies that succeed at that task—rather, it focuses on the lessons that his character, moral fiber, and faith have to offer us in this woefully overmanaged but underled culture.

The first section affords a quick overview of the great man's life. It traces his triumphs and tragedies with an eye toward understanding how he was able to weave a fabric of lifelong success in accord with the glad tidings of providence.

The second section focuses on thirty essential character traits that typified Roosevelt's career, relationships, and habits of life. What were the disciplines of mind and morals, what were the priorities of heart and soul, what were the passions of spirit and flesh that drove him to such heights as he attained?

Finally, in the third section, the lessons of Roosevelt's great legacy are examined in light of the needs of our own time. How can we learn from him to answer the challenges of today?

Generally, today we hold to a strangely disjunctive view of the relationship between life and work—thus enabling us to nonchalantly separate a person's private character from his public accomplishments. But this novel divorce of root from fruit, however genteel, is a ribald denial of one of the most basic truths in life: what you are begets what you do. Wrongheaded philosophies stem from wrongheaded philosophers; yet orthodoxy invariably begets orthopraxy. Sin does not just happen; it is sinners that sin. Likewise, heroes do not simply emerge ex nihilo; heroes are forged upon the anvil of ethical faithfulness.

English historian and journalist Hilaire Belloc noted, "Biography always affords the greatest insights into sociology. To comprehend the history of a thing is to unlock the mysteries of its present, and more, to discover the profundities of its future."[15] Similarly, the inimitable Samuel Johnson quipped, "Almost all the miseries of life, almost all the wickedness that infects society, and almost all the distresses that afflict mankind, are the consequences of some defect in private duties. Likewise, all the joys of this world may be attributable to the happiness of hearth and home."[16]

Or, as E. Michael Jones has asserted, "Biography is destiny."[17]

It is my prayer that the example of Theodore Roosevelt portrayed within these pages will inspire a whole new generation of emerging leaders to attain to their destiny.

Chronology

We are better for the lives and deeds of our mighty men who have served the nation well.[18]

1858 Theodore Roosevelt is born in New York City on October 27.

1865 With his brother and childhood friend Edith Carrow, Theodore watches the funeral cortege of Abraham Lincoln from his parlor window.

1868 His parents take the entire family on a grand tour of Europe.

1875 His homeschooling experience concludes with a year of special tutoring in Latin, Greek, and mathematics—disciplines that figured prominently in the college entrance examinations of the day.

1876 He is accepted at Harvard College and takes rooms nearby in Cambridge.

1880 He graduates from Harvard University on June 30.

   He marries his Harvard sweetheart, Alice Lee, on October 27.

1881 He briefly studies law at New York University before deciding to enter public service.

1882 He is sworn in as the youngest New York state legislator.

   On a hill overlooking Oyster Bay on Long Island he builds a house—resplendent with porches and porticoes and brimming with his disposition and personality—later to be named Sagamore Hill.

Written for the most part while in college, his first book, *The Naval War of 1812*, is published.

1883   After leading a successful legislative campaign to reform judicial and civil service appointments, he is reelected by the widest margin of any New York legislator.

1884   On February 14, both his wife and his mother tragically die—his wife while giving birth to his first child, Alice.

In grief, he heads west to work on his cattle ranch in the Dakota Territory.

1886   He returns home and conducts an unsuccessful campaign for mayor of New York.

He marries Edith Carrow on December 2.

1887   His biography of Thomas Hart Benton is published.

On September 13 his first son, Ted Jr., is born.

1888   His long-awaited biography of Gouverneur Morris is published.

1889   He is appointed as a U.S. Civil Service commissioner and moves to Washington.

The first volume of *The Winning of the West* is published.

On October 10 his second son, Kermit is born.

1891   His history of New York City is published to rave reviews.

On August 13 his second daughter, Ethel, is born.

1894   On April 10 his third son, Archie, is born.

On August 14, after a long history of drinking, his brother Elliot dies in a tragic fall.

1895   He resigns his post in Washington to become president of the New York Police Board.

He coauthors *Hero Tales from American History* with Henry Cabot Lodge.

1897   He is appointed assistant secretary of the navy by President William McKinley.

On November 19 his fourth son, Quentin, is born.

1898 Commissioned an army colonel, he raises a volunteer cavalry (the famed Rough Riders) to fight in the Spanish-American War.

He returns from the war as a hero and is overwhelmingly elected governor of New York on November 8.

1900 He is unanimously chosen to join incumbent William McKinley on the Republican ticket and is elected vice president on November 4.

His book *The Strenuous Life* is published and becomes a bestseller.

1901 President McKinley is shot on September 6 by an assassin while attending the Pan American Exposition in Buffalo.

After appearing to make a quick recovery, the president succumbs to his wounds. Roosevelt is sworn in as his successor in September 14.

His biography of Oliver Cromwell is published.

1902 His carefully researched scientific treatise *The Deer Family* is published.

He successfully negotiates a settlement to a national coal strike.

1903 He dramatically enforces the Monroe Doctrine against European encroachment in Venezuela—winning for himself hero status throughout Latin America.

He recognizes the secession of Panama from Columbia and initiates construction of the Panama Canal.

1904 On November 8 he is reelected by the widest popular margin ever recorded by a presidential candidate.

1905 He secures the first workmen's compensation and employer's liability laws.

1906 On February 17 his daughter Alice marries Congressman Nicholas Longworth in a magnificent White House ceremony.

After masterminding the peace treaty ending the Russo-Japanese War, he is awarded the Nobel Peace Prize.

He outlines the solution of the Algeciras Conference, bringing peace to indigenous North Africans and the European colonial powers.

1907   He establishes the Roosevelt Foundation for Industrial Peace.

He launches a historic around-the-world naval flotilla—the first circumnavigation of the globe by a national naval force.

1909   He retires to private life upon the expiration of his presidential term.

On March 23 he sets sail for an African safari and a grand tour of Europe.

1910   He serves as special ambassador to England at the funeral of King Edward VII.

He returns from abroad to discover that his successor in the White House, William Taft, has compromised many of his most important policies and reforms.

1911   He becomes an editor for *Outlook* magazine.

1912   The publication of his book *Conservation of Womanhood and Childhood* launches a national movement resulting in new child and family labor laws.

On February 25 he announces his candidacy for the presidency.

Though he had won all but one primary and caucus, his delegates are barred from the Republican National Convention by the party establishment. The lackluster incumbent is renominated.

Breaking with the Republican Party, he is nominated by the fledgling Progressive Party on August 7 and begins a vigorous campaign.

Leading slightly in the polls, he is wounded in an assassination attempt on October 14 and is forced to sit out the vital final three weeks of the race.

He easily outdistances Taft; however, Democratic rival Woodrow Wilson ekes out a win on election day November 5 with 41 percent of the vote.

1913   He embarks on a daring hunting and exploring adventure in the Brazilian Amazon where he is seriously injured and contracts malaria—complications from which he will suffer for the rest of his life.

1916 His prophetic book *Fear God and Take Your Own Part* is published.

1917 He requests sanction to raise a volunteer battalion to fight in the First World War, but is denied permission by Wilson.

1918 All four of his sons are deployed on the German front.

In February, Archie is seriously wounded.

In July, Quentin is shot down behind enemy lines and dies—although immensely proud, he never fully recovers from the grief.

1919 He dies at Sagamore Hill on January 6.

1925 Congress approves Gutzon Borglum's plan for a massive sculpted memorial at Mount Rushmore to America's greatest statesmen—George Washington, Thomas Jefferson, Abraham Lincoln, and of course, Theodore Roosevelt.

Who goes there? An American!
Brain and spirit and brawn and heart,
'Twas for him that the nations spared
Each to the years its noblest part;
Till from the Dutch, the Gaul, the Celt
Blossomed the soul of Roosevelt.

Student, trooper, and gentleman
Level-lidded with times and kings,
His the voice for a comrade's cheer
His the ear when the saber rings.
Hero shades of the old days melt
In the quick pulse of Roosevelt.

Hand that's molded to hilt of sword;
Heart that ever has laughed at fear;
Type and pattern of civic pride;
Wit and grace of the cavalier;
All that his fathers prayed and felt
Gleams in the glance of Roosevelt.

Who goes there? An American!
Man to the core—as men should be.
Let him pass through the lines alone,
Type of the Sons of Liberty.
Here, where his fathers' fathers dwelt,
Honor and faith for Roosevelt.[19]

Grace Duffle Boylan

THE
Courage
and Character of
THEODORE
ROOSEVELT

The Life of
Theodore Roosevelt

*Speak softly and carry a big stick; you will go far. It
sounds rather as if that were but a homely old adage, yet
as is often the case with matters of tradition, this truism is
actually true.*[1]

A Bull Moose

I feel as fit as a Bull Moose.[2]

AT A CAMPAIGN STOP in Milwaukee on the evening of October 14, 1912, a deranged, out-of-work bartender emerged from a crowd and shot Theodore Roosevelt in the chest at point-blank range. Staggered by the impact of the bullet and the shock of the injury, the great man nevertheless righted himself.

As the crowd converged on the man, the wounded former president cried, "Stand back! Don't hurt the man! Bring him to me!" After examining his would-be assassin with a dismissive glare, he told his aides to get him to the rally. "This may be the last speech I deliver," he admitted. Seeing that he was bleeding heavily, several doctors in Roosevelt's party wanted to rush him to the hospital at once, but he waved them aside. "You just stay where you are," he ordered. "I am going to make this speech and you might as well compose yourselves." When they persisted, he said, "Get an ambulance or a carriage or anything you like at ten o'clock and I'll go to the hospital, but I won't go until I've finished my speech." He then demanded that his driver proceed to the auditorium and said fervently, "I will make this speech or die. It is one thing or the other."[3]

When he reached the rally, the emcee announced that an attempt had been made on Roosevelt's life. But as he appeared on the platform, the familiar figure smiled and waved weakly to the awestruck crowd. "It is true," he whispered in a hoarse voice, "I have just been shot. But it takes more than that to kill a Bull Moose."[4]

Now beginning to gain his composure, he said, "Friends, I should ask you to be as quiet as possible. And please excuse me from making a long speech. I'll do the best I can." He then took his manuscript from his jacket; it had been pierced through by the bullet and was soaked with blood. "It is nothing," he said as the people gasped. "I am not hurt badly. I have a message to deliver and will deliver it as long as there is life in my body." The audience became deathly still as he went on to say, "I have had an A-1 time in life and I am having it now."[5]

He always had the ability to cast an intoxicating spell over crowds. Even now, his physical presence was dominating. His charisma was infectious. His passionate commitment to what he believed was right and good and true was dynamically compelling—even to those who opposed him politically.

Though by then he was bleeding profusely, he spoke for an hour and a half—waving off repeated appeals for him to stop and seek medical treatment. By the end he had almost completely regained his typical stump fervor—rousing the crowd to several extended ovations. When at last he allowed his concerned party to take him to the hospital, the audience reached a near frenzy chanting "Teddy! Teddy! Teddy!"

At the hospital he joked and talked politics with his attendants. But his condition was hardly a joking matter. The surgeons found that the bullet had fractured his fourth rib and lodged close to his right lung. "It is largely due to the fact that he is a physical marvel that he was not mortally wounded," observed one of them later. "He is one of the most powerful men I have ever seen on an operating table. The bullet lodged in the massive muscles of the chest instead of penetrating the lung."[6]

Nevertheless, he was no longer a young buck at fifty-four. He was required—against his quite considerable will—to sit out the remainder of the campaign. Still, he lived to fight another day.

Later his biographers viewed the incident as quintessential Roosevelt: imposing the sheer force of his will upon a seemingly impossible circumstance and prevailing.[7] From beginning to end, that was the story of his life. He was forever defying the odds, defying all reason, defying the very physical realities of life in this poor fallen world.

A Slow Start

*I was a sickly, delicate boy, suffered much from asthma,
and frequently had to be taken away on trips to find a
place where I could breathe.*[8]

THEODORE ROOSEVELT JR. WAS born on October 27, 1858, in New
York City. His father, Theodore Roosevelt Sr., was a sixth-generation
New York burgher—the scion of one of the richest and most influen-
tial old Dutch families of Manhattan. By all accounts he displayed an
exuberant, disciplined, and masculine joy of life. The child's mother,
Martha Bulloch Roosevelt, was an unmistakable southern belle—
the beautiful and delicate daughter of one of the most prominent
Scottish plantation families of Georgia.

This child was the heir of two proud traditions that he would
cherish for the rest of his life: the sturdy Dutch industrial mercantilism of the North and the romantic Scottish pioneer agrarianism of
the South. Nicknamed Teedie, he grew up in a harmonious home
where Yankee vigor and ingenuity was balanced by Dixie refinement
and sophistication, masculine discipline by feminine gentleness, intellectual seriousness by intellectual inquisitiveness, the rewards of
privilege by the responsibilities of charity, and the bustle of urbanity

by the decorum of gentility. Into this happy home were shortly added two more siblings—a sister and a brother—so there was no lack of activity or companionship.

Two things, however, contrived to disturb Teedie's early idyllic existence. The first came five months after his second birthday. Despite repeated promises to withdraw threatening troop placements, President Abraham Lincoln suddenly ordered a massive reinforcement of the federal garrison at Fort Sumter—situated in the strategic harbor of Charleston, South Carolina. As a result, hostilities erupted between North and South. The bitter war not only divided the land, it divided the Roosevelt household. Teedie's mother and his Bulloch grandmother and aunt (who had come to live with the young family in New York) were unrepentant Confederate sympathizers. They participated in clandestine relief efforts—sending contraband supplies across the blockaded lines—and kept in full communication with other Bulloch family members who were actively involved in the makeshift Rebel military operations aimed at repulsing any and all Northern invaders. Indeed, they gaily hung the Stars and Bars from eaves of their midtown brownstone following the many Southern victories at the beginning of the conflict.

Teedie's father, on the other hand, was a passionate Unionist and a loyal Lincoln Republican. Though he could not in good conscience take up arms against his beloved Confederate in-laws, he was actively engaged in the Federal war effort—working on behalf of the enlisted men on the front lines. For many months he lobbied in Washington to secure legislation designed to provide financial stability and security for families the soldiers had left at home. Afterward, he tirelessly sloughed through the mud of the freezing camps, urging paymaster reforms and bolstering Yankee morale.

The long absences from the family that these activities required were especially felt by his young son. From the moment of his father's departure, Teedie's health began a precipitous decline. This was the

second trial that contrived to disrupt his bucolic childhood. He suffered from an unceasing barrage of ailments and conditions—all
somewhat related to congenital asthma, which the family generically
called *cholera morbus*. His little body was continually wracked by
coughs, colds, nausea, and chronic diarrhea. His younger sister later
related, "Rarely, even at his best, could he sleep without being
propped up in bed or a big chair."[9] His gauntness and fragility re-
minded his mother of the pale withering azaleas of early summer.
And it was whispered that he probably would not live to see his
fourth birthday.

The return of his father from the war was a tonic to the whole
family. And while Teedie took a turn for the better, he continued to
suffer poor health throughout his childhood. He was often confined
as an invalid for months at a time. And his earliest memories were
of fitful nights gasping for a breath of air while both of his parents
hovered about his sickbed.

During his long convalescences he benefited from the tales and
reminiscences of his parents and grandparents. They would regale
him with stories, legends, and songs from the past. They would fill
his mind with florid romance, dashing adventure, and a fierce sense
of his proud heritage that would ever after shape his consciousness.
Later he continued to feed his voracious appetite for such things,
becoming a lifelong avid reader.

His father, concerned that Teedie's sickly body would never
allow him to enjoy the kind of full life he constantly read about, at
last confronted him with the issue. "Theodore," the big man said,
"you have the mind but you have not the body. And without the
body the mind cannot go as far as it should. You must *make* your
body. It is hard drudgery to make one's body, but I know you will
do it."[10]

His mother later remembered her son's reaction was the half-
grin, half-snarl that later became world famous. Jerking his head

back, Teedie set his jaw and replied, "I'll make my body. By heaven, I *will*."[11]

Indeed, he did. With bulldog tenacity he began to make daily visits to a local gym to lift weights, to box and spar, and to compete in gymnastic exercises. Later he installed a small gym in the second-floor piazza off his bedroom, where he literally beat his body into submission.

Precocious Youth

*While still a young boy I began to take an interest in
natural history. I remember distinctly the first day that I
started on my career as a zoologist.*[12]

IN FURTHER ATTEMPTS TO strengthen his frail son's body, Theodore
Sr. began to take his family each spring and summer to the rugged
shores of Oyster Bay on Long Island. There Teedie and the other
children learned to appreciate the joys of nature. They swam along
the beach, rode horses up and down the rolling hills, hiked through
the woods, hunted in the meadows, fished in the streams, and rowed
across the bay. They built wigwams at the edge of the forest, gathered
hickory nuts and wild apples, climbed to the tops of the tallest trees,
and scampered down long, leafy foot trails.

Despite his incessant illness, Teedie seemed to have an inexhaustible fund of energy. He could hardly be kept still—even when
sorely afflicted by one of his debilitating asthma attacks. His many
hours of enforced reading combined with his keen powers of observation in the woods quickly combined to make him something of a
prodigy. He became a serious student of natural history—keeping detailed journals and notes of his sagacious studies of local flora and

fauna. By age seven he had begun a little museum containing a carefully indexed and classified collection of insects, bird nests, rocks, minerals, and cocoons. And by the time he was nine, his repertoire of specimens had expanded to snakes, rodents, birds, and small mammals. He even began to learn the technical processes of taxidermy.

When the family embarked on a year-long grand tour of Europe in 1869, Teedie's intellectual proclivities became particularly pronounced. He not only reveled in the art and architecture, history and pageantry, chivalry and nobility of the Continent, he was fascinated by its spectacular natural beauty. From the dales of England to the forests of Germany, from the mountains of Switzerland to the valleys of the Rhine, from the highlands of Lombardy to the lowlands of Belgium, Teedie was bedazzled by the infinite variety of creation.

His diaries indicate a mind capable of astonishingly prodigious recall and insatiable appetites. Already, historian Edmund Morris pointed out, the contours of his interests and character were in evidence: "Promptness, excitability, warmth, histrionics, love of plants and animals, physical vitality, dee-light, sensitivity to birdsong, fascination with military display, humor, family closeness, the conservationist, the historian, the hunter—all are here."[13]

While Teedie attained marked intellectual growth, his conscience was also pricked by the poverty and deprivation he had witnessed abroad. His father was either the founder or an early supporter of virtually every cultural, humanitarian, and philanthropic endeavor in the city of New York. His unceasing efforts to establish the New York Orthopedic Hospital, the Children's Aid Society, and the Newsboys' Lodging House had already made a deep impression on his son. Theodore Sr. was instrumental in organizing the Protective War Claims Association, the Soldiers' Employment Bureau, and the Blackwell's Island Sanitarium Society. The founding meetings of the American Museum of Natural History and the Metropolitan

Museum of Art were both called by him and held in the family's front parlor. And he made certain that the life and fellowship of the Madison Square Presbyterian Church were central priorities for the family—not only on Sundays when he taught a mission class, but throughout the week. As a result, young Teedie had a ready context within which to develop his newly awakened concerns.

Toward the end of 1872 the Roosevelts embarked on yet another foreign adventure—one even more adventurous than their previous grand tour of Europe. In addition to long sojourns in England, Germany, and Italy, they visited the Middle East—including Palestine, Syria, and Egypt. It was on this trip that all of the disparate aspects of Teedie's wide-ranging interests—books, history, scientific observation, the outdoor life, and Christian social concern—began to be fully integrated into a cohesive world view. As his father related, "He went away a boy and returned a young man."[14]

The Harvard Dandy

I thoroughly enjoyed Harvard and I am sure it did me good, but only in the general effect, for there was very little in my actual studies which helped me in after life.[15]

HOMESCHOOLED BY HIS VERY capable Bulloch aunt, Teedie gained a rich classical education—studying the sundry general liberal arts of literature, history, music, theology, and philosophy, the venerable trivium disciplines of grammar, logic, and rhetoric, as well as the various quadrivium derivatives of German, French, astronomy, biology, architecture, and geometry. By the time he was fifteen, he was well versed in the Western canon of classical literature—from the golden age of pagan antiquity to the glorious flowering of Christendom, and from the precipitous dawning of the Reformation to the ominous disconsonance of the Enlightenment. He was particularly knowledgeable in the area of military and political biography—he drank deeply from the wells of Virgil, Plutarch, Augustine, Cato, Athanasius, Eusebius, Seneca, Machiavelli, Samuel Johnson, Edmund Burke, Thomas Carlyle, and Thomas Macaulay.

Despite this great breadth and depth of intellectual acumen, he was sorely deficient in several areas of great importance. If he were to be admitted to Harvard—where he longed to pursue his interests in natural science and history—he would have to vastly improve his skills in Greek, Latin, and mathematics. A tutor was secured for this purpose, and just as he had determinedly set out to "make his body," he now focused on "making his mind."

In 1876 he passed the rigorous entrance exams and enrolled in the prestigious school. His father sent him off with the sage counsel, "Take care of your morals first, your health next, and finally your studies."[16] He did just that.

Though he tackled a full academic course load, he immediately engaged himself in a number of extracurricular activities designed to fulfill the greatest hopes and expectations of his parents. He taught a Sunday school class at Christ Episcopal Church in Cambridge. He began to publish a series of serious articles on various scientific, social, and political subjects. He became an avid participant in the school's intramural athletics program. And he joined the rifle club, the natural history club, the finance club, and the elite Porcellian Club. He also nurtured a wide range of social relations—thus establishing friendships he would maintain throughout his life and career.

Though he was considered by his classmates as a dandy and a raconteur because of his stylish dress and confident demeanor, he was anything but. In fact, everything he was and everything he did was animated by his devotion to his family and by his determination to maintain their esteem. He told his mother that, because of them, "I have never spent an unhappy day unless by my own fault."[17] And he wrote his father, "I do not think there is a fellow in College who has a family who love him as much as you all do me. I am sure that there is no one who has a father who is also his best and most intimate friend, as you are mine. I have kept the first letter you wrote me and shall do my best to deserve your trust."[18]

Sadly, his blissful existence was to be shattered during the winter term of his second year at Harvard. His father, though only forty-six and always a paragon of vim, vigor, and vitality, was stricken with what was diagnosed as acute peritonitis—but which was actually a virulent strain of stomach cancer. In less than two months he was dead.

Suddenly called home from school, Teedie found the entire city in mourning—with flags flown at half-mast and black bunting draped across the crenelations of the public buildings. Lauded in *Harper's Weekly*, Roosevelt Sr. was described as an "American citizen of the best type—cheerful, hearty, sagacious, honest, hopeful; not to be swerved by abuse, by hostility, or by derision." His father was sorely missed by all who knew him. Though inconsolably stricken with grief, young Roosevelt, as the eldest son, had to act the part of the head of the house.

When he returned to school after the funeral, he was determined more than ever to uphold the honor of his name. "How I wish I could ever do something to keep up his name."[19] To that end, he vowed to "study well, finish Harvard, and carry on like a brave Christian gentleman."[20]

Fairy Tale Love

There is no joy that hurts so well as young love.[21]

THE NEXT SUMMER, YOUNG Roosevelt's relationship with Edith Carrow blossomed into a serious romance. Playmates, best friends, and sweethearts since they were toddlers, no one was surprised when they became all but inseparable. They went rowing, sailing, hiking, and picnicking together. By all accounts they were perfect for one another—not only sharing a passionate interest in books, ideas, science, and charitable concerns, but balancing one another's temperaments: where he was "ardent and impulsive, feverish in his enthusiasms, she was sensitive and cautious, a cooling breeze over his sometimes overheated landscape."[22]

But then one afternoon they apparently quarreled bitterly. They broke off their relationship in a fit of fury—and would hardly see one another for years afterward. Brokenhearted, Roosevelt returned to Harvard.

Less than two months later though, he met another beautiful young lady—and suddenly all rueful thoughts of Edith's lost love were banished. Alice Lee was the seventeen-year-old daughter of a prominent Boston banking family. Fair, flirtatious, radiant, and viva- cious, Alice was quite popular with the privileged sons of New Eng- land gentry as well as the bright young men of Harvard. But from the moment he laid his eyes on her, Roosevelt would countenance no challenge to his determination to "marry that girl."[23]

With all the ardor that seemed to attend everything he under- took in life, Roosevelt began to court Alice. During the next weeks and months, he used all of his considerable charms to win her heart—though he recorded in his diary that he had "asked God's help in staving off temptation and to do nothing [that he] would have been ashamed to confess" to his father.[24]

Amazingly, he was able to maintain his excellent grades—and in his senior year he juggled his relentless pursuit of Alice with his many extracurricular activities. He was elected to the Hasty Pudding Club. He was asked to preside over the finance and natural history clubs. He vied for the lightweight boxing championship—ultimately win- ning the silver medal. And he began an ambitious project of writing an authoritative book about the naval history of the War of 1812.

Though she resisted for some time, in the end, Alice was won over completely by his boundless energies, enthusiasms, and affec- tions. On January 25, 1880, she consented to marry him. Roosevelt was ecstatic. The final semester whirled past as he made joyous preparations for their new life together.

There was, however, one dark cloud hanging over his happy exis- tence. And he told no one about it—not even his beloved Alice— until the very end of his life. Shortly before graduation, he had a complete physical examination. The results were alarming. The doc- tor had detected a frighteningly erratic heartbeat and warned the young man to choose a sedentary occupation—he even advised him to avoid all physical exercise, including going up and down stairs, if he wished to enjoy a long life.

Typically, Roosevelt quickly retorted, "Doctor, I am going to do all the things you've told me not to. If I must live the sort of life you have described, I don't care how short it is."[25] Shortly afterward he emphasized his resolve by mountain climbing in Maine. Later that summer he embarked on an exhausting six-week hunting expedition to the West with his younger brother.

On October 27, 1880, he married his "sweet, blue-eyed queen" Alice. At the reception following the simple ceremony, the sunshine, champagne, and merriment generated such euphoria that even Edith Carrow—who of all the guests had the least reason to celebrate—happily "danced the soles off her shoes."[26] For once the verbose Roosevelt was utterly speechless in the thrall of his fairy tale romance. He noted tersely in his diary, "Our intense happiness is too sacred to be written about."[27]

A Reformer's Zeal

What is politics for if not to right wrongs and to stand for truth?[28]

AFTER A BRIEF HONEYMOON at Oyster Bay, the newlyweds settled in New York where Roosevelt had enrolled at the prestigious Columbia University Law School. He was still somewhat uncertain about his future, but he had determined that whatever course he might eventually take, a study of the law would prove to be beneficial.

He plunged into his studies with his usual fervor, but he quickly found he needed more of a challenge than his professors could provide. So each afternoon following a full schedule of classes he would plunge into his research and writing for *The Naval War of 1812.* Upon publication, the book was immediately heralded as a "formidable literary achievement"[29] and the "harbinger of a great new historical talent."[30] This was indeed remarkable—especially considering its author was a mere twenty-three years old and had begun the project while still an undergraduate. A century after its first appearance, *The Naval War of 1812* remains a standard work on the subject on both

45

sides of the Atlantic—and a required text at the U.S. Naval Academy at Annapolis.

Meanwhile his romance with Alice continued unabated. They enjoyed a wide circle of friends and were quickly swept into a swirl of social engagements. Roosevelt was only too happy to show off his beautiful wife. With his scintillating and controversial mind and her stunning and gracious presence, they became the talk of the town in no time.

With the acclaim that attended the successful launch of his publishing career and the attention that accompanied his stellar social rise came the interested scrutiny of various political forces within the city. Indeed, Roosevelt had already involved himself in various local controversies and had become an active member of his neighborhood Republican Club—making his mark as an unabashed advocate of political reform. It was probably inevitable that opportunity-seeking reformers in the corrupt, machine-dominated city should put his name forward as a possible candidate for the state assembly. Tired of the party establishment's incessant back-room wheeling and dealing, the delegates at his precinct caucus surprisingly disregarded the experienced incumbent and nominated the young upstart in 1882.

Not long afterward, Roosevelt outlined his political philosophy in his journal, writing that he would be a "strong Republican on state matters, but an Independent on municipal matters."[31] Thus, at the very beginning of his career, he signaled a principled tension between party loyalty, on the one hand, and singular independence, on the other—a tension that was to dominate his life in politics ever after.

Much to the alarm of his backers, he had a tendency to speak his mind. Nevertheless, his constituency found his honesty a refreshing departure from politics as usual. He won easily—becoming the youngest member of the New York Assembly.

As historian Nathan Miller has observed, "Theodore Roosevelt burst upon Albany with the same effect he had at Harvard and within a few months became one of the most prominent figures in New York politics."[32] He delivered his maiden speech a few days after arriving at the capital. The assembly was deadlocked concerning the competing claims of two Democratic rivals for the speakership. Upon learning that several Republicans were discussing the possibility of throwing their support to one or the other in order to expedite the business of government, Roosevelt leaped to his feet to object on the grounds that it was good politics to let the Democrats tear themselves apart. "As things are today in New York, there are two branches of Jeffersonian Democrats," he declared. "Neither of these alone can carry the state against the Republicans. Clearly then, we have no interest in helping one section against the other." He went on to assert, "While in New York City, I talked with several gentlemen who have large commercial interests at stake. They do not seem to care whether the deadlock is broken or not. In fact, they seem rather relieved. And if we do no business until the end of the session, I think the voters of the state will get along quite well without it."[33]

The press lauded his combination of brash conservatism and reformist zeal as "the most refreshing new development in New York politics in decades" and "the voice of a new era in American statesmanship."[34] And thus a star was born.

During the next several months Roosevelt led an odd coalition of mugwumps, progressives, and reform-minded conservatives in a firebrand crusade to clean up the state's corrupt judicial and civil service spoils systems. There was much at stake—vast wealth and tremendous power were wielded by the entrenched political bosses. Not surprisingly then, virtually none of the pundits or prognosticators of the day gave Roosevelt any real chance of success. Though they privately may have admired his brave attempt to restore civic virtue, they publicly derided it as little more than an idealistic and quixotic quest, doomed to failure.

Nevertheless, despite his youthful inexperience, lack of any substantive political base, and innumerable threats against his life and well-being, the sheer force of his energy, courage, and tenacity somehow secured one legislative victory after another. Though the changes he had wrought were modest, he had suddenly come to symbolize the hope of reformers everywhere.

Again and again Roosevelt declared his political credo was simply "to take out of politics the vast band of hired mercenaries whose very existence depends on their success, and who can almost always overcome the efforts of them whose only care is to secure pure and honest government."[35] It was not exactly the kind of credo designed to win over the confidence of the political establishment. But it did gain for him a faithful following among the masses—a following that would remain dedicated to him throughout his long career. During the next two election cycles his constituents rewarded his integrity and selfless courage with the widest reelection margins of any legislator in New York.

Tragedy

Life brings sorrows and joys alike. It is what a man does with them—not what they do to him—that is the true test of his mettle.[36]

SOME THREE YEARS AFTER their marriage, Alice became pregnant. Roosevelt was thrilled. He desperately wanted children—longing to create for them the kind of family life he had enjoyed as a child. Alice, too, was delighted.

Immediately they both turned their attentions to the house they planned to build on a grassy hilltop overlooking Oyster Bay on Long Island. Roosevelt had already purchased nearly a hundred acres there and had engaged architects to design a "spacious home with a multitude of gables, dormers, windows, chimneys, and a sprawling wraparound porch" where he and Alice and their brood of children could sit on rocking chairs and contemplate the sunset.[37] With ten bedrooms, a comfortable gentleman's library, and facilities for gracious entertainment, the house was to be a quite a grand endeavor—well beyond the means of the young couple. But then Roosevelt rarely tackled a project that was sensibly within his means.

Distracted by the call of duty back in Albany, Roosevelt was forced to leave Alice several times during her pregnancy—much to the distress of both of them. Each day he wrote tender letters to her expressing his deepest affections: "I have to read my Bible all to myself, without my pretty queenie standing beside me in front of the looking glass combing out her hair. There is no pretty, sleeping rosebud face to kiss and love when I wake in the morning."[38]

Despite the joyous anticipation of his firstborn, he was deeply concerned for his delicate wife. And for good reason. Alice was not having an easy time of it. Because of her frail constitution she was forced to spend much of the pregnancy in bed. All of the regular distresses of child-bearing—from nausea and swelling in the joints to back pains and severe abdominal cramping—were magnified for her.

When she went into labor prematurely, Roosevelt was away at the capital. Happily though, on February 12, 1884, Alice safely delivered a healthy eight-and-three-quarter-pound baby girl.

But then the real trouble began. The telegram sent to Roosevelt the next morning noted that, while the baby was in good health, the mother was "only fairly well." A few hours later he received another message ominously bidding him to return to New York "immediately."[39]

When at last he reached home, he was met by his distraught brother with dire words: "There is a curse on this house. Mother is dying and Alice is dying too."[40] The doctors had diagnosed Alice as suffering from Bright's disease—a severe renal ailment that had gone undetected throughout her pregnancy. Martha Bulloch Roosevelt, who had fallen ill with what appeared to be a cold a few days before, was diagnosed as suffering from the final stages of typhoid. The two people dearest to him in all the world were now on the threshold of death—at the same time and in the same house.

Roosevelt rushed up the stairs and disconsolately held Alice in his arms for several hours while she hung on to life by a slender thread. He was beckoned downstairs where his mother was drawing her final breaths. Sometime after midnight she died, and Roosevelt ran back up the stairs to Alice. His vigil continued through the long night and into the next afternoon, when at last Alice too died. It was St. Valentine's Day. Alice was just twenty-two years old.

Two days later Roosevelt sat in the front pew of the Fifth Avenue Presbyterian Church—where he and Alice had worshiped together so many times—for the double funeral. The next day the family was back in the same pew for the baptism of Roosevelt's little daughter. She was christened Alice Lee.

Later he would write in his journal, "The light has gone out of my life."[41]

Go West Young Man

*In after years there shall ever come to mind the memory
of endless prairies shimmering in the bright sun; of vast,
snow-clad wastes, lying desolate under gray skies; of the
melancholy marshes; of the rush of mighty rivers; of the
breath of the evergreen forest in summer; of the crooning
of ice-armored pines at the touch of the winds of winter;
of cataracts roaring between hoary mountain passes; of
all the innumerable sights and sounds of the wilderness
and of the silences that brood in its still depths.*[42]

THE SHOCK OF HIS tragic loss, as well as a series of disconcerting
political machinations within the Republican Party, combined to
entirely demoralize Roosevelt. Reevaluating all of his priorities, he
resolved to leave his old life in New York behind and make a career
out west in the wide open ranges of the Dakota Territory. Leaving
his infant daughter with his sister, he sold off most of his possessions and departed for his season in the wilderness—both literally
and figuratively.

During the previous two years he had been cautiously investing
a portion of his inheritance from his father in a cattle ranch overlooking a bend in the Little Missouri River. With a couple of his old
hunting and tracking cronies from Maine, he decided to manage his
investment on site.

Though he could not have known it at the time, it may well
have been the most astute political decision he ever made—or ever
would. Historian Nathan Miller asserted:

Roosevelt had three major liabilities in politics: he was an aristocrat, he was an intellectual, and he was an easterner. Altogether, he spent only about three years in the Badlands, a period interrupted by sometimes lengthy stays in the East. Yet he so successfully identified himself with the West that for the remainder of his life, the public thought of him as a rough-riding cowboy rather than a New York dude. This western experience removed the stigma of effeminacy, ineffectuality, and intellectualism that clung to most reformers.[43]

Even so, his move west was anything but image-conscious posturing. He had every intention of staying there for the rest of his life. And in short order he won the respect of the rough-and-tumble men of the frontier by his unflinching courage, his unfailing honesty, and his unfettered enthusiasm for the land. Sometimes with his fists, sometimes with his gun, but most often with his cunning, he carved out a new and satisfying life for himself among them. In addition, he was a quick study and gained their approval as a skilled rancher.

His long, arduous days on the cattle trail were often followed by equally long, arduous nights with pen and paper. Roosevelt turned his many western adventures into a series of well-received books— which included *Hunting Trips of a Ranchman*, *Ranch Life and the Hunting Trail*, *The Wilderness Hunter*, and a biography of the western expansionist, Thomas Hart Benton.

Reviewers lauded the works as "masculine, fervid, and innovative."[44] Indeed, the books sparked a whole new interest in the issues of the range and the lifestyle of the rugged frontiersman. They dramatically brought the world of the rancher to life with vivid descriptions of the land, the people, and its wildlife. They essentially created a whole new genre of literature. With the novels of his old friend and Harvard classmate Owen Wister and the art of Frederic Remington, his books helped to generate the great American legend and lore of the "Wild West."

Of course, the wildness of the West was not simply legend and lore. Roosevelt alone had enough genuine adventures with bucking broncos, grizzly bears, and desperadoes to certify it as such.

In one his most famous escapades, Roosevelt tracked two petty thieves for three days across more than a hundred miles of wilderness. Battered by a howling wind and subzero temperatures, he nevertheless brought them to justice—traveling another six days and 150 miles downstream to do so.

Now it appeared he was a genuine American hero and not a "pasteboard figure made by the artifice of politics and wealth."[45]

Destiny Fulfilled

Happy homes are the responsibility of husbands and fathers—but inevitably it is wives and mothers who make it so.[46]

WHEN HE AT LAST returned to New York, his friends and acquaintances were amazed by his dramatic transformation. It was almost as if his lifelong struggle against illness and frailty, as well as his more recent struggle against grief and despair, were suddenly crowned with an unexpected victory. The anemic and dispirited dandy who had left the city had returned rugged, bronzed, and in the prime of health.

Indeed, his whole demeanor was changed. According to one observer, "There was very little of the whilom dude in his rough and easy carriage."[47] Even his crisp, clipped New York accent had been smoothed into the easier, relaxed tones of the frontier. His old friend William Thayer, who had not seen him for several years, was astonished "to find him with the neck of a Titan and with broad shoulders and a stalwart chest."[48] He speculated that "this magnificent specimen of manhood" would have to spend the rest of his life "struggling to reconcile the conflicting demands of a powerful mind and an equally powerful body."[49]

One day shortly after his conspicuous return, he met Edith Carrow coming down the stairs of his sister's house. For nearly seven years he had managed to almost completely avoid her. But his childhood sweetheart had remained his sister's closest friend— and while he was away, she had been a regular visitor in the Roosevelt household.

He now discovered that in the intervening years she had become alarmingly attractive. Rejecting any and all potential suitors—at the risk of becoming an old maid—she had matured into a complex figure of femininity and loveliness.

Against his will, he was utterly smitten.

During the next several weeks they began to see more and more of each other. Though driven by a sense of guilt—he somehow believed that he was being untrue to the memory of Alice—Roosevelt asked Edith to marry him. She accepted without hesitation; she had always loved him and no other.

After a quick trip back to his ranch to settle a few business affairs, he returned to the East to stay. His original plan was to make a living with his scientific writing and journalism. But politics would simply not leave him alone.

No sooner had he unpacked his bags than several influential New York Republicans urged him to accept the party's nomination for mayor. There was little chance of winning—the election was a mere three weeks away and had already attracted two other well-financed candidates. But they believed that the young Roosevelt could make a strong showing, thus establishing a precedent for the borough balloting to be held later in the year.

Roosevelt accepted the challenge and entered the fray with his usual enthusiasm. Known as the "Cowboy Candidate," he worked eighteen-hour days, appeared at four or five rallies every night, and won over the city's typically jaded media. Indeed, the *New York Times* exuded, "He excites more confidence and enthusiasm than has been inspired by any candidate in a mayoralty contest within the memory of this generation of voters."[50]

In the end, though he had surprisingly made a real race out of it, Roosevelt was defeated. His heroic last-minute stumping was simply too little, too late—though he had certainly proven his popular appeal to the power brokers and kingmakers in the party establishment.

A few days later, Roosevelt, his sister, and Edith boarded a steamer and set sail across the Atlantic. The couple would fulfill what each of them believed to be their providential destiny.

On December 2, 1886, Theodore Roosevelt and Edith Carrow were married in a quiet, private ceremony at St. George's Church, Hanover Square, in London.

A Political Quest

*The worst enemies of the republic are the demagogue and
the corruptionist.*[51]

FOLLOWING A LEISURELY HONEYMOON in Europe, the Roosevelts
moved into the newly completed but never-inhabited house at Oyster Bay—now dubbed Sagamore Hill. Believing his political career,
for all intents and purposes, to be finished, Roosevelt turned his energy toward establishing his literary reputation.

First, he wrote a biography of Gouverneur Morris, the master-
mind behind the first draft of the Constitution. The book was remarkable for its clarity of vision and its applicability to the
contemporary political scene. Roosevelt obviously had that essential
conservative trait of being able to find immediate lessons for the
present from the past.

He also began work on a masterful multivolume history entitled
The Winning of the West. It was to be a sweeping drama of the hero-
ism, hardship, warfare, and struggle that made the conquest of the
North American continent not only possible but inevitable.

He dug deeply into original sources, and his research was meticulous—although he completely rejected the modern German-inspired notion of academic history as a kind of social science. Instead it was a branch of literature. "History," he argued, "should be a work of art and imagination rather than a dry compendium of facts."[52] He was an unashamed moralist who wholeheartedly believed that it was the duty of the historian to make value judgments to draw immediate and applicable lessons for the contemporary reader. The result was a remarkably fresh perspective on the American story—one as vibrant as the events themselves.

His books received rave reviews; it appeared he would indeed be able to support his growing family—Edith had five children in quick succession during the next few years—with his pen.

Once again though, Roosevelt's quiet respite from the hubbub of politics was short-lived. When Republican Benjamin Harrison won the presidency in 1888, Roosevelt was tapped to fill one of three Civil Service Commission positions in the new administration.

Roosevelt gave his all in all to this rather unglamorous but vitally important position. Before long he had transformed the sleepy little department into the locus of reform in the federal government. Once again it was Roosevelt against the forces of corruption, recalcitrance, and cronyism—only this time, it was a part of his job description. He was charged by the new president to completely restructure the way jobs in the vast federal bureaucracy were doled out.

Always a skilled tactician, he was careful to fulfill that mandate while at the same time keeping the ruling coalition intact and in charge. And that was no mean feat. For years the spoils system had been the means by which politicians paid their debts to supporters—rather than making appointments based on any system of merit. Thus, cushy federal offices had become the corrupt currency of political life. Obviously, there were entrenched forces determined that their vested interests were left undisturbed. That meant Roosevelt had to face off against some of the most ruthless men in the country. He thought that sounded "just bully."[53]

For the next four years his efforts catapulted the dull cause of civil service reform onto the front pages of the newspapers—and propelled Roosevelt into the national limelight. In fact, he became such a powerful and popular voice for government integrity and efficiency that when the Republicans lost power in the next election, the new Democratic administration wisely decided that they could ill afford to replace him. He was the only Republican officeholder to be so retained.

Though flattered by the new administration's recognition of his accomplishments, Roosevelt no longer felt challenged by the job. So when the opportunity arose to take the job of New York City's police commissioner, he jumped at the chance.

Once again he was cast in the role of a reformer. This time, instead of trying to manage the vast federal bureaucracy, he was to rid the nation's largest and most important police department of graft, corruption, and inefficiency—and there was plenty "to get rid of."[54]

A sullen indolence had come to dominate the force. The department was run as a kind of personal fiefdom by the political machine in the city. Officers were "on the take" in virtually every borough. Prostitution rings, gambling cartels, drug smuggling cabals, and protection rackets operated with impunity.

Roosevelt quickly modernized the entire system of operations—introducing such innovations as forensics, fingerprinting, rap sheets, and investigative departments—thus pioneering standard police procedures that have remained in use to this day. He walked the beats himself—often alone at night—in an effort to catch officers who were sleeping on the job, shaking down the citizenry, or engaging in other illegal activities. He restructured the entire chain of command and instituted a system of merit that completely altered the character of the criminal justice system around the nation.

His phenomenal successes once again thrust him into the national limelight. Though he was only thirty-seven years old, his name was often mentioned in connection with the presidency. His star was definitely on the rise.

Meanwhile, despite such a flurry of public activity, Roosevelt had settled into an immensely happy family life. He was by all accounts an ideal father. His children adored him—and he gave himself to them with complete abandon. Edith often complained that she actually had seven children to contend with—not six. But he was also a devoted husband. Not only did he remain head over heels in love with her, he was careful to keep their relationship his first priority— even amid so many other pressing responsibilities.

Given his incredible public productivity and his private penchants, one New York socialite quipped with no little exasperation, "How can anyone possibly be that perfect? Surely there is dirt under the corner of the carpet somewhere." Edith quickly responded, "Not a speck."[55]

Rough Rider

There is nothing more for me to do here in Washington. I've got to go into the fight myself.[56]

THE NEXT NATIONAL ELECTIONS brought the Republicans to power once again and Roosevelt yearned for a strategic appointment that would enable him to do more than simply clean up the messes others had made. He wanted to be a constructive reformer rather than always being cast in the role of a critical reformer.

Ever since writing *The Naval War of 1812* he had been an advocate of building a strong navy—a stance that had not been incorporated into American defensive strategy since the War Between the States. In addition, he had become increasingly convinced that a showdown was imminent between the old colonial powers of Europe and the United States. Thus he sought for an appointment as undersecretary of the navy. His rationale was simple: "I want to be where the action is."[57]

After a brief hesitation—President William McKinley's advisers were somewhat cautious about Roosevelt's independent streak—he won his coveted prize and went to work with his typical ardor. He quickly mastered the technical details of running a modern navy and became an expert in everything from munitions and armor plating to blast trajectories and fuel efficiency ratings. His boss, the former governor of Massachusetts, John Long, was entirely uninterested in such details. That suited Roosevelt. After all, that meant he was essentially left to run the navy as he saw fit—within congressional guidelines, of course.

At the time, the fleet was a small, uncoordinated, and dilapidated force that served as little more than a ceremonial coast guard. It ranked well behind the navies of Britain, France, Germany, Spain, Russia, and Japan—with only four first-class battleships, two armored cruisers, and forty-eight other vessels of various types, ranging from harbor tug boats to small torpedo launches. Roosevelt embarked on an aggressive campaign to expand and modernize the fleet. He also drew up strategic plans to better coordinate the resources already at hand should war come with one of the great powers.

And he was convinced that it would come. He was particularly concerned about Spain. The old colonial behemoth was engaged in quashing rebellions all across its wide-flung empire—in the Philippines, in Puerto Rico, and most seriously, in Cuba. Reports of fierce oppression had stirred American public opinion against the Spanish, and administration concerns about the obstruction of international commerce had rankled the ire of Congress. Thus Roosevelt readied his department as best he could for what he was convinced would be a nasty confrontation.

As it turned out, Roosevelt's instincts were all too prescient. He secured the promotion of Com. George Dewey to commander of the Asiatic Squadron, supplied him with a strategy for the conquest of Manila Bay, and placed him on war readiness. Similarly, he outlined a Caribbean strategy that would isolate Spanish interests and bring independence to Cuba.

President McKinley—cautious as always—wanted to avoid the pretext for war at all costs. Thus he ordered a large armored cruiser, the *Maine*, to make a "courtesy visit" to Havana from Key West, its port of call. A few weeks later, while the *Maine* lay peacefully at anchor in Havana Harbor, an explosion ripped through the hull of the American vessel. Casualties were heavy—266 of the 354 crew members were killed. Although an investigation of the blast failed to reveal direct Spanish complicity, war now seemed inevitable.

Roosevelt's mobilization plans were quickly implemented—and ultimately proved to be the decisive difference in the war. Meanwhile, he had resigned his position with the navy after winning a commission to command a volunteer detachment of troopers on the front lines of battle.

All who knew him tried to dissuade him from what appeared to be a foolhardy and unnecessary risk. Even McKinley argued that his influence would be greater if he would stay in Washington. As if that were not enough, Edith was recovering from a life-threatening illness—and he had his own troop of six children at home to care for.

But nothing could keep him away from the action. "If I am to be any use in politics," he said, "it is because I am supposed to be a man who does not preach what he fears to practice. For the last year I have preached war with Spain. I should feel distinctly ashamed if I now failed to practice what I have preached."[58]

The regiment Colonel Roosevelt was to command was composed of a thousand men—some Eastern dandies, some Western cowboys, and only a handful of experienced soldiers. Nevertheless, they were whipped into fighting shape quickly—at a camp near San Antonio, Texas—and shipped to the front lines. In less than a month and a half Roosevelt had taken them from raw recruits to an efficient fighting force.

On June 22, 1898, the Rough Riders—as they had been dubbed by the popular press—landed on the pristine beaches some twenty miles from the strategic city of Santiago. In short order they were involved in several fierce fire fights with the seasoned Spanish defenders. Movement was treacherous and slow. Even so, Roosevelt demonstrated coolness and bravery under fire and quickly earned the respect of his men. He advanced his corps over the next several days toward Santiago. On July 1 they were in position for a charge up the last hill for a final assault on the heavily fortified Spanish garrison.

Like Shakespeare's Henry V before the battle of Agincourt, Roosevelt moved among his men, lending them hearty encouragement and checking on last-minute contingencies. For as long as he lived, he looked back on that day as "the greatest of my life."[59] And it was indeed glorious. The assault was successful. Casualties, though heavy, were fewer than expected.

Roosevelt was no less heroic after the great battle than he was during it. He seemed everywhere—securing essential provisions, opening direct communications for officers back home, coordinating the inefficient quartermastering, and maintaining high morale among the enlisted men. And he even secured early release of the troops once the Spanish crown had officially capitulated. He seemed to cast a spell of reverence and awe wherever he went.

The commander of the overall operation, Gen. Joseph Wheeler, recognized Roosevelt's vital role in the victory and recommended him for the Medal of Honor. But the people of the United States accorded him an even greater honor—they garnered him with universal praise and adulation. Only thirty-nine years old, Col. Theodore Roosevelt, commander of the Rough Riders, was now the most famous, the most admired, and the most popular man in America—bar none.

A Political Accident

We worked very hardy but I made a point of getting a
couple of hours off each day for equally vigorous play.[60]

Roosevelt RETURNED HOME TO discover a bevy of political oppor-
tunists seeking his favor and attention. A group of independent reformers, progressives, and mugwumps wanted him to consider
starting a national third-party movement. A group of influential Republicans desired him to run for Congress. Another group wanted
him to run for governor. Still another group wanted him to consider
challenging the Republican presidential nomination.

Weighing his options carefully, he decided the wisest course for
the present was to seek the gubernatorial prize. His closest friend and
political adviser, Henry Cabot Lodge, concurred. If his goal was
eventually to reach the White House, there was no better stepping-
stone than the governor's mansion in Albany—five of the seven
presidential races since the War Between the States had featured either a sitting governor or a former governor.

Campaigning on a simple platform of "courage," an "upright ju-
diciary," and "honesty in government," Roosevelt captured the moral
high ground early in the contest. The result was never in doubt.

In keeping with his view of limited government and principled conservatism, his administration was most noted for its efforts to bring about bureaucratic efficiency, managerial economy, tax reform, and meritorial advancement in the civil service. He continually appealed for practical morality and manly virtue in the civic arena. "It is absolutely impossible," he declared, "for a Republic long to endure if it becomes either corrupt or cowardly."[61]

His accomplishments as governor were impressive. They included banning local option school segregation, securing the rights of workers to choose whether or not to unionize, bringing about sweeping municipal reform to New York City, and establishing the first statewide tax reform code banning property seizures without jury trials.

As always, he was a hive of activity in his private life—and he had a knack for keeping himself in the public eye even when he stepped away from his official duties. He wrote a bevy of articles and books. He gave an enormous number of speeches. He traveled to every corner of the state. He kept the pace of his outdoors activities and his scientific endeavors. He remained faithfully involved in his local church—still teaching in his Sunday school class as often as possible. And of course, he plunged headlong into the myriad activities of his bustling young family.

Not surprisingly, when Vice President Garret Hobart died unexpectedly, a ground swell of support from all across the nation put Roosevelt's name at the top of the list of candidates to replace him on the Republican ticket for 1900. Though President McKinley was cool to the idea at first—again, fearing Roosevelt's impetuously independent streak—he at last consented.

It was a good thing he did, too. The Republican convention that summer was like a coronation party for Roosevelt. As the center of attention, he was actually quite resistant to the notion of becoming vice president. He was afraid it was a political dead end rather than the opportunity of a lifetime. In fact, several of his fiercest rivals supported the idea of placing him on the ticket because they believed it would sufficiently sidetrack his career and keep him safely away from the action.

But the convention delegates would not entertain Roosevelt's objections, and he was nominated unanimously on the first ballot.

President McKinley chose a front-porch campaign strategy—he did not venture out to even a single rally, assembly, or meeting during the race. Thus the full weight of the election stumping was left to Roosevelt. Once again his boundless energies and unflagging enthusiasms served him well. He gave hundreds of speeches and traversed nearly twenty-five thousand miles. According to the press, the real story of the campaign could be adequately summed up in the words of a popular ditty: "'Tis Teddy alone that's running, and he ain't just running, he's galloping."[62]

In the end, the Republicans won their greatest victory since the time of Reconstruction.

Roosevelt, despite the great role he had played in the election victory, was rather despondent once the dust had settled. "The Vice President is really a fifth wheel to the coach," he groused. "It is not a stepping stone to anything but oblivion."[63] In fact, his service in the active part of his new office lasted only four days.

During the summer congressional recess, he took advantage of the opportunity to spend some time at Sagamore Hill, go hunting, fishing, hiking, and climbing with his family in New England, and catch up on his reading—during the campaign he had drastically cut down his reading to a mere three or four books a week. He made a point to simply enjoy life to the fullest.

At the end of the summer President McKinley was winding up a two-day visit to the Pan American Exposition in Buffalo, New York. It was a lavish world's fair that dramatized the great cultural, scientific, economic, and industrial strides American had taken in the previous century.

The president was greeting well-wishers in a reception line when a young anarchist stepped out of the crowd and shot him at point-blank range. Roosevelt rushed to his bedside; for the first several days it appeared he might well recover. By September 10, four days after the shooting, McKinley seemed to be entirely out of danger and Roosevelt was told his departure from Buffalo would help assure the nation that the crisis was finished. But then on September 13, the president suddenly took a turn for the worse. Within twenty-four hours he was dead.

At the time Roosevelt was climbing remote Mount Marcy—the highest peak in the Adirondacks—with several close friends. They were on their way down from the exhausting climb when they were intercepted by a park ranger with the news. The men quickly hiked to the nearest telephone—about a dozen miles away—where they picked up a security detachment and a buckboard for the forty-mile ride to the nearest train station.

Somber and apparently lost in his thoughts, Roosevelt barely spoke to anyone during the arduous journey. His train was mobbed by newsmen all along the way—but he remained in seclusion. He did not comment, in fact, until after he had taken the oath of office in Buffalo. Then he simply asserted:

> The administration of the government will not falter in spite of the terrible blow. It shall be my aim to continue, absolutely, unbroken, the legacy of President McKinley for the peace, the prosperity, and the honor of our beloved country.[64]

At forty-two, Theodore Roosevelt was now the youngest president in American history. And though he had arrived at the White House by accident, he had indeed arrived.

TR: Rex

No man ever enjoyed being president more than I did.[65]

THEODORE ROOSEVELT WAS BORN to be president of the United States. Once the American citizenry had recovered from the shock of McKinley's assassination, Roosevelt's presence in the White House seemed somehow natural, comfortable, even inevitable. He exuded a charismatic confidence that immediately set people at ease.

Nearly everything he did seemed to break new ground—and yet his progressive innovations and reforms all naturally grew out of his fiercely conservative Christian principles. He created a brouhaha when he invited famed educator Booker T. Washington to the White House for dinner—the first African American to have such a privilege. He mandated equal pay for equal work in all federal offices—the first legal protection for female workers. He ordered the Justice Department to investigate any violations of the Sherman Antitrust Act—passed in 1890 but never consistently enforced. And he announced to the colonial powers that he would forcefully prosecute any territorial encroachments under the authority of the Monroe Doctrine—again, long before enunciated but never before enforced.

In short, Roosevelt determined that at least with his administration, "The government should simply say what it means and mean what it says."[66] The public endorsed his program of honest government and the rule of law with solid Republican victories in the midterm elections of 1902. His influence from the "bully pulpit" of the White House was felt far and wide.

As historian Nathan Miller noted:

In little more than a year in office, Roosevelt had captured the imagination of the American people. He had launched the Square Deal, brandished the Big Stick against the trusts, personally settled a major coal strike and won the support of labor and the public, enlarged the power and prestige of his office, and emerged as the leader of the Republican party. He had shown the will and skill to capitalize on the opportunities that came his way.[67]

During the next two years leading up to the 1904 elections, Roosevelt continued to cement his mythic status. By negotiating the end of the devastating Russo-Japanese War, he not only became the first American to win the Nobel Peace Prize, but also established the United States as a genuine international power and an arbiter of peace. Many had feared that his course of military preparedness and aggressive stance on foreign affairs would inevitably lead America down the path of war; instead, his was the most conflict-free administration in history. Not a single shot was fired against a foreign foe and not a single engagement was seriously threatened at any time during his seven and a half years in office—though there were a few tense moments about European debt collection in revolution-wracked Venezuela, the acquisition of the Canal Zone in Panama, and the broad intent of the Monroe Doctrine. It appeared that the president's "Big Stick" policy was indeed a roaring success.

The election campaign of 1904 was practically a formality. He ultimately won by a landslide. Nevertheless, he worried about the outcome throughout the campaign. When the returns came in on election night, he was thunderstruck with emotion. "I am stunned by the overwhelming victory we have won. I had no conception that such a thing was possible. I had thought it probable we should win, but was quite prepared to be defeated. But of course, I had not the slightest idea that there was such a tidal wave of support."[68] He quipped to Edith, "My dear, I am no longer a political accident."[69]

During his second administration his popularity only soared to greater and greater heights. Unfortunately for him, that did not necessarily translate into legislative success. Much of his policy agenda was ignored by a lackadaisical Congress—not so much out of substantive opposition as out of indolent satisfaction with the status quo. As a result, he grew more and more restless as the months and years passed.

Perhaps that is why he stuck to his guns about not running for a third term. There was no constitutional provision to prevent it—and there was little doubt that he would be easily reelected if he chose that course. He maintained his self-imposed lame duck status nevertheless.

Apart from the construction of the Panama Canal, a determined fight against segregated schools, and the dramatic strengthening of the national parks and forests system, his final months in office were essentially ceremonial. Perhaps his most significant achievement in those final days was the selection of his successor. And in that he made a dastardly error—or so he later thought.

He designated his secretary of war as his heir apparent. A 350-pound former Ohio Supreme Court judge, William Howard Taft hardly cut the same heroic figure as Roosevelt. But all he needed to gain the nomination and win the election was a nod from the president. And that he got.

Though the nation cried out for "four more years," Roosevelt was resolute.[70] During the Republican convention, delegates pledged to Taft staged an hour-long demonstration in an attempt to somehow convince the president to change his mind. Even after Taft's nomination, spontaneous rallies on behalf of Roosevelt cropped up across the nation. In the end though, he ensured that his dour and corpulent friend would indeed succeed him. Taft was elected, though—everyone agreed—only as the proxy of the great man who had preceded him.

On March 4, 1909, Theodore Roosevelt and his family left the White House with a round of bittersweet farewells.

A Restless Heart

I do not number party loyalty among my commandments.[71]

IMMEDIATELY AFTER LEAVING OFFICE, Roosevelt left the country for a year-long safari in Africa, followed by a grand tour of Europe with his family. The trip included hunting, reading, conducting scientific experiments, hiking, and swimming. In short, he did all the things he so dearly loved to do—the things that the press of public responsibility had prevented him from doing over the past several years.

But he had an ulterior motive for his long absence. "My main reason for wishing to go to Africa for a year," he confided to friends, "is so I can get where no one can accuse me of running, nor do Taft the injustice of accusing him of permitting me to run the job."[72] He wanted to give Taft a chance to make his own way.

Alas, it quickly became apparent that Taft instead lost his way.

From weeks-old newspapers and letters from friends, Roosevelt learned his successor was bungling the job—and that already he was on the verge of tearing asunder the successful Republican coalition Roosevelt had worked so hard to pull together.

Taft had cast a languid sleepy spell over the government in Washington—yielding to the whims and wiles of Wall Street industrialists and big-city machine bosses. It was not a happy contrast with the man who had preceded him in office. Taft was a decent man; there was no disputing that. But he seemed to lack vision. Though he had a brilliant legal mind and vast foreign policy experience, he appeared bland and inarticulate. He seemed to have no ideas of his own—and even those he did have seemed muddled. By all appearances, he epitomized an entrenched and institutional politics as usual. He had unwittingly allowed the White House to become captive to powerful vested interests. He was a follower, not a leader.

Meanwhile, Roosevelt was wrapping up his successful safari with a round of visits with the sundry kings, emperors, presidents, and prelates of Europe. At Cambridge, where he delivered a major scientific paper, he was introduced as "the peer of the most august kings, queller of wars, destroyer of monsters wherever found, yet the most human of mankind, before whose coming comets took to flight, and all the startled mouths of seven-fold Nile took flight."[73] Thus the contrast between the two men was only heightened. Dissatisfaction with Taft became pandemic.

Life magazine heralded the return of Roosevelt to America:

> Teddy, come home and blow your horn,
> The sheep's in the meadow, the cow's in the corn.
> The boy you left to tend and keep,
> Is under the haystack fast asleep.[74]

Although he attempted to avoid commenting publicly on the domestic strife now brewing in Washington, privately he began to express genuine concern that Taft might undo all the good he had accomplished during his administration. When he arrived in New

York on June 18, 1910, the pressure to jump into the fray became almost irresistible.

Whistles shrieked, horns blew, salutes were fired, and the largest crowd ever gathered in one place on American soil greeted Roosevelt's return. He was at the zenith of his popularity. It was a brilliant, sunny day.

But the storm clouds were gathering.

Gradually, in the next several weeks and months, the contrast between Roosevelt and Taft was transformed into a genuine conflict of ideals. Eventually, Roosevelt felt he had to speak out and oppose the direction in which his old friend had chosen to lead the nation.

That was a fateful decision. According to Henry Cabot Lodge, "That one decision may well have altered the course of our nation's history—indeed the history of the whole world—more than any other single decision in the course of the last fifty years."[75]

Indeed, it may well have.

1912

My hat is in the ring.[76]

OF ALL HIS ADVENTURES and accomplishments, Roosevelt's involvement in the presidential race of 1912 was perhaps his most significant—and certainly his most controversial. That year the electorate was confounded by a whole host of dire dilemmas. The lackluster Taft administration had created a real conundrum for voters.

The fiery Democratic nominee was Woodrow Wilson. Though he had served briefly—and without notable distinction—as governor of New Jersey, Wilson was essentially a political unknown. And yet, because the campaign hinged on the issue of change, anything seemed possible.

According to Wilson, change was essential. "Our life has broken away from the past," he said.[77] "Old political formulas do not fit the present problems."[78] He believed: "This is nothing short of a new social age, a new era of human relationships, a new stage setting for the drama of life."[79] He was convinced that the "new age" demanded "new circumstances" and the "fitting of a new social organization."[99] He wanted to "bring the government back to the people" through an aggressive implementation of activist legislation, adjudication, and administration.[81] He advocated radical change: "Politics in America is a case which sadly requires attention. The system set up by our law and our usage doesn't work—or at least it cannot be depended on."[82]

He boasted that Americans had an obligation to reinvent the world by "interpreting the Constitution according to the Darwinian principle" and by becoming "architects in our time."[83] He foresaw the advent of "a glorious New World Order" and "a marvelous New Freedom."[84]

Because Taft seemed either unwilling or unable to deflect Wilson's energetic barrage of ideological rhetoric, Theodore Roosevelt reluctantly came out of retirement and took to the stump. He decried the liberalism of Wilson saying that the nation should be "ruled by the Ten Commandments" not "by Darwinian presumption."[85] He claimed that "the great heart of the nation beats for truth, honor, and liberty," and thus he felt compelled to decry "the immorality and absurdity" of Wilson's "doctrines of socialism."[86] He asserted that he was an "old school conservative" who believed in "the progressive notions" that made for "a strong people and a tame government."[87]

Taft was chagrined. He fought back with a derisive negative campaign. He accused his old friend Roosevelt of "reckless ambition."[88] He chided his old boss of "unsettling of the fundamentals of our government" and called him a "serious menace and an extremist."[89]

Roosevelt handily won the hearts of the grass roots and secured nine out of every ten electable delegates sent to the national convention. However, he was eventually denied the Republican nomination through a series of last-minute back-room maneuvers by key members of the party establishment—who were afraid they would not be able to control the always independent-minded Roosevelt.

Scandalized and demoralized, the Republicans divided—the "moderates" stood by Taft while the "progressives" remained loyal to Roosevelt. The fractious campaign would be a three-way race—with the popular Roosevelt leading a fledgling third-party effort.

The politics-as-usual finagling, mudslinging, and conniving outraged the popular press and exacerbated the electorate. Disaffection with the entire process ran rampant. Roosevelt angrily charged:

> The old parties are husks, with no real soul within either, divided on artificial lines, boss ridden and privilege controlled, each a jumble of incongruous elements and neither daring to speak out wisely and fearlessly what should be said on the vital issues of the day.[90]

As the campaign progressed, it appeared that Roosevelt's last-minute third-party challenge might actually defy all odds and succeed. Though he had virtually no money, no organization, and no political apparatus behind him, his sheer popularity and force of will threatened to carry the day.

But then, with less than three weeks to go, Roosevelt was the victim of an assassination attempt. Though his wound was not mortal, he was unable to return to the rigors of the campaign. Uncertainty suddenly gripped the electorate. Torn between the two old familiar parties and the one national leader they could trust, voters were frozen in indecision. They stayed away in droves.

On election day, ambivalence reigned. None of the candidates received a majority. Though Wilson attained a weak plurality against Roosevelt, and was thus declared the winner, nearly 60 percent of the popular vote had actually gone against him. As a result, he entered the White House the next year without any semblance of a mandate, facing a formidable array of opposition forces.

Roosevelt, on the other hand, though somewhat discouraged by the outcome, took solace in the fact that he had overcome the odds;

with little more than public affection on his side—he was outspent by each of his opponents by more than ten-to-one—he had very nearly toppled the supremacy of the two establishment parties.

He was still only fifty-four years old. Nevertheless, he felt certain that he had heard his "last hurrah" in the rough-and-tumble world of politics.[91]

Years of Exile

Better faithful than famous.[92]

I HAVE TO GO. It is my last chance to be a boy."[93] With those words Roosevelt launched the most dangerous wilderness expedition of his long and remarkable career as an outdoorsman. Finding the radical posturing and preening of the Wilson administration difficult to face, he had arranged to join an expedition to map the unexplored River of Doubt, which flowed though the heart of Brazil's dense Amazonian rain forest.

It was to be a dangerous and harrowing expedition—fighting off everything from fierce fire ants and giant red wasps to aggressive piranhas and poisonous reptiles. The explorers disappeared into the dense wilderness for more than two months. During the journey two men were lost as well as five of their seven canoes and most of their supplies and provisions. Most members of the expedition contracted dysentery and malaria—including Roosevelt and his son Kermit.

When the party at last emerged from the jungle, having successfully mapped the fifteen-hundred-mile-long river, they discovered they had been given up for dead. Roosevelt had lost fifty-seven pounds and severely injured his leg. He would never fully recover. And he returned to a world that was about to engage in a war from which it would never fully recover either.

As the regional Balkan hostilities began to escalate into the First World War during the summer of 1914, Roosevelt was transformed into a kind of prophet in the wilderness. He believed Americans would ultimately be drawn into the war and ought to therefore prepare themselves against that day. Once again his instincts were startlingly accurate. But this time his was an unwelcome message. Americans were in an isolationist mood—and they believed, against all evidence to the contrary, that preparedness might actually draw them into the widening conflict. Though he was personally as popular as ever, the public, on the whole, refused to heed Roosevelt's dire warnings—until it was too late.

He wrote books, made speeches, lobbied his old allies in Washington. But he was branded a warmonger, an extremist, an alarmist. Like Winston Churchill would be in the years prior to the Second World War, Roosevelt was vilified by isolationists and accommodationists alike. But he never wavered in his convictions, and his voice refused to be drowned out by the din of public opinion.

When at last his prediction of American involvement in the war was fulfilled, each of his four sons, as well as one son-in-law, immediately volunteered. Roosevelt himself sought to raise and lead a division into battle—just as he had during the Spanish-American War. But President Wilson would hear none of it—that was the last thing the beleaguered president needed: Theodore Roosevelt leading a heroic charge across the battlefields of Belgium and France.

Feeling somewhat vindicated by the turn of events, Roosevelt led the war effort at home. He helped the sale of bonds. He made speeches to raise morale. He lobbied for better provisioning. His star seemed, at last, on the ascendancy again. Americans began to look upon their old hero for a sense of direction in such disconcerting times. The Republican Party even began to entertain the idea of putting his name forward to lead their ticket in 1920.

But on July 16, 1918, Roosevelt learned his youngest son had been killed in a aerial dogfight over German lines. His stoic exterior belied the devastation he and Edith felt. Issuing a public statement he said, "Quentin's mother and I are very glad that he got to the front and had a chance to render some service to his country, and to show the stuff that was in him before his fate befell him."[94] Later he asserted, "Only those are fit to live who do not fear to die; and none are fit to die who have shrunk from the joy of life and the duty of life."[95]

In truth, Quentin's death somehow broke Roosevelt's heretofore indomitable spirit. During the next six months, the nagging effects of his malaria and recurring bouts of inflammatory rheumatism and gout hobbled him time and again. Though he remained as busy as ever standing for the cause of reform—prompting Republican leaders to continue to promote him for the 1920 ticket—he was obviously suffering a serious physical decline. At long last, it appeared that he had worn out his body. He was in and out of the hospital several times during the winter.

Doctors let him go home for Christmas—but with a warning. They threatened that he might well be confined to a wheelchair for the rest of his life if he didn't slow down. Of course he had no intention whatsoever of slowing down. He retorted crisply, "All right then. I can work that way, too."[96]

Two weeks later, on January 5, 1919, he worked on several articles before retiring fitfully to bed. Before drifting off to sleep he told Edith, "I wonder if you will ever know how much I love Sagamore Hill."[97] At about four o'clock the next morning, an old friend staying at the house became alarmed at Roosevelt's irregular breathing. He called for a nurse, but before anyone could arrive Roosevelt stopped breathing. Edith was awakened and rushed to her husband's side. "Theodore, darling," she called to him softly. "Theodore, darling."[98] But there was no reply.

"The old lion is dead,"[99] was all the cable read that was sent later that morning.

Vindication

Weasel words from mollycoddles will never do when the day demands prophetic clarity from greathearts.[100]

THE FUNERAL OF Theodore Roosevelt was a quiet family affair at Oyster Bay within sight of his beloved Sagamore Hill home. It was there, accompanied by the hushed strains of his favorite hymn, George Keith's "How Firm a Foundation," that he was laid to rest.

But America—indeed the world—would not be content with such a private end to such a public life.

Hundreds, perhaps even thousands, of memorial services were held across the land. Messages of grief, sorrow, and condolence poured in from around the globe—from kings and princes to paupers and pedestrians. Accolades, eulogies, tributes, and reminiscences were published, broadcast, and announced at every turn. It seemed everyone, from the mighty to the obscure, desired to have their say about the great man.

On February 9, 1919, a memorial service was held in Congress—and afterward a reverent prayer vigil was held. Henry Cabot

Lodge, his dearest friend, closest confidant, and political mentor, spoke in halting tones of a man like no other man any of them had ever known:

> He had a touch of the knight errant in his daily life, although he would have never admitted it; but it was there. It was not visible in the medieval form of shining armor and dazzling tournaments but in the never-ceasing effort to help the poor and oppressed, to defend and protect women and children, to right the wronged and succor the downtrodden. Passing by on the other side was not a mode of travel through life ever possible to him; and yet he was as far distant from the professional philanthropist or the liberal do-gooder as could well be imagined, for all he tried to do to help his fellow men he regarded as a part of the day's work to be done and not talked about. No man ever prized sentiment or hated sentimentality more than he. He preached unceasingly the familiar morals which lie at the bottom of both family and public life. The blood of some ancestral Scotch Covenanter or of some Dutch Reformed preacher facing down tyranny was in his veins, and with his large opportunities and vast audiences he was always ready to appeal for justice and righteousness. But his own particular ideals he never attempted to thrust upon the world until the day came when they were to be translated into realities of personal action.[101]

He concluded, saying:

> Indeed the absolute purity and integrity of his family life—where those ideals first met the test of authenticity—tell us why the pride and interest which his fellow countrymen felt in him were always touched with the warm light of love. In the home so dear to him, in his sleep, death came, and . . . so, Valiant-for-Truth passed over and all the trumpets sounded for him on the other side.[102]

Whether poet, bard, jester, or knave, it seemed the world's testimony of him was but one:

> He dwelt with the tribes of the marsh and moor,
> He sat at the board of kings;
> He tasted the toil of the burdened slave
> And the joy that triumph brings.
> But whether to jungle or palace hall
> Or white-walled tent he came,
> He was brother to king and soldier and slave,
> His welcome was the same.[103]

But of all the things said about him in the days and weeks following his sudden death, the greatest tribute to Theodore Roosevelt's legacy of service came from the political arena—as he would have wished.

Woodrow Wilson proved to be a supremely unpopular president. He acted decisively to implement his radical agenda—four constitutional amendments were passed that revolutionized the nature of American governance—and he was able to concentrate vast new powers in the hands of the central government. However, Wilson was never able to win popular support. Though he had somehow survived a tepid reelection bid, virtually all of his proposals and policies were met with ignominious defeat. Even his proposals for the cessation of hostilities following the First World War, his famed Fourteen Points and the League of Nations, were repudiated at home.

By the end of Wilson's second term, the whole conception of activist government had been thoroughly repudiated. The president was mired in scandalous unpopularity. His administration was a disaster. The world was in shambles following the war. And the peace of Versailles portended even worse. Democracy had done all that socialism had threatened to do.

The electorate realized that it must rally from its dismal and equivocal mindset. And so it did.

Warren G. Harding, the conservative Republican candidate, issued a clarion call for a return to "normalcy." He said:

> America's present need is not heroics, but healing; not nostrums, but normalcy; not revolution, but restoration; not agitation, but adjustment; not surgery, but serenity. The world needs to be reminded that all human ills are not curable by legislation, and that quantity of statutory enactment and excess of government offer no substitute for quality of citizenship.[104]

America was ready for a return to the quiet certainty that, while politics is important, it is not all-important. Voters had to abandon their natural reticence and ambivalence. They realized that sometimes political involvement must take precedence in our lives in order to ensure that political involvement does not take preeminence over our lives. They had learned that lesson the hard way.

They gave Harding a landslide victory. Ultimately though, it was a victory for Roosevelt—the platform the Republicans ran on was virtually identical to the one he had espoused just a few years prior. Harding ran self-consciously as a "Roosevelt Republican."[105]

Even as Roosevelt's image was being carved into the face of Mount Rushmore—joining the pantheon of America's greatest men—the impress of his leadership was again looming large over the land.

"He being dead yet speaketh."[106]

The Character of
Theodore Roosevelt

It is not the critic that counts; not the man who points out
how the strong man stumbles, or where the doer of deeds
could have done better. The credit belongs to the man who
is actually in the arena, whose face is marred by dust and
sweat and blood; who strives valiantly, who errs, and
comes short again and again, because there is no effort
without error and shortcoming; but who does actually
strive to do the deeds.[1]

His Family

I have had the happiest home life of any man I have ever known.[2]

THEODORE ROOSEVELT FOUND HIS greatest joy not in power, fame, wealth, or even adventure but in his family. There is much about his life and career that may be open to dispute, but on this issue there can be little doubt. According to his own testimony, it was his family that was the source of his strength, the locus of his vocation, and the wellspring of his values:

> No other success in life—not being President, or being wealthy, or going to college, or anything else—comes up to the success of the man and woman who can feel that they have done their duty and that their children and grandchildren rise up to call them blessed.[3]

At a time when the Victorian family ethic was still very much in vogue—positing that children should be seen and not heard and that domesticity was a singularly feminine concern—Roosevelt was notable for his dissent. He loved his home life—and all that attended it.

He was a hopeless romantic who wrote affectionate letters to Edith on an almost daily basis. He regularly sent her flowers, adorned her with jewelry, and made certain that they had time alone together regardless of his hectic schedule. She was his best friend, his confidante, and his lover. He fully believed "the greatest privilege, the greatest duty for any man is to be happily married."[4] And he was.

But it was his relationship with his children that best demonstrates the priority he placed on family life. Visitors to Sagamore Hill or the White House always were amazed by both the exuberance and the predominance of the great man's participation in "childish things."[5] He often postponed important affairs of state to play with the children. He taught them to swim and hunt and row and sail and ride. He often took them on what he dubbed his "rambles and romps" through the woods—a rigorous beeline hike that made no compensation for hills, fences, streams, or undergrowth.

Once the Japanese ambassador was surprised to discover the president on his hands and knees roaring down the hallway outside the Oval Office and chasing a gaggle of squealing children—a real live teddy bear. A distinguished British guest staying in the Lincoln bedroom was awakened late one night by a rambunctious game of touch football up and down the White House corridor. Right in the middle of the ruckus was, much to his dismay, the American president.

Roosevelt allowed the White House to be turned into a regular menagerie of strange pets. At various times the children enjoyed the presence of a lion, a hyena, a coyote, several bears, an owl, kangaroo rats, flying squirrels, rabbits, and guinea pigs. And of course, the White House stables featured a goodly variety of ponies, donkeys, thoroughbreds, and even a zebra. It was a child's paradise.

All four of his boys idolized him. Both of his daughters believed him to be their knight in shining armor. His oldest child, Alice, once asserted that he was "a King Arthur, a William Wallace, and a Buffalo Bill all rolled into one."[6] When his youngest son, Quentin, was asked by a White House journalist to describe the president in a single word, he quickly responded. "Fun," he said. "Papa is fun."[7]

Of course, Roosevelt was not all fun and games. He was a strict disciplinarian who tolerated many things—but disrespect, disobedience, and discourtesy were not among them. He took it upon himself to be the enforcer of the family standards—he filled their lives with good books, great ideas, marvelous adventures, and open affections. He taught them the catechism and conducted family devotions—albeit sporadically—from the time they were very small.

He believed that private life was the proving ground for public life. "A man must do well in his own home," he argued, "before he can do well outside."[8] To be certain, he practiced what he preached.

As they grew into adulthood, he became for his children a beloved intimate. His letters to them were published as paragons of the ideal family. Not surprisingly, each child carried the standard of his father's faith and ideals throughout their lives. It would be difficult—indeed, altogether impossible—to comprehend all that he was and all that he did apart from this unshakable commitment to his family. For Theodore Roosevelt, family values were the essential foundation stones for all other values:

> There is need to develop all the virtues that have the state for their sphere of action; but these virtues are as dust in a windy street unless back of them lie the strong and tender virtues of a family life based upon the love of the one man for the one woman and on their joyous and fearless acceptance of their common obligation to the children that are theirs.[9]

His Father

My father was the best man I ever knew. He combined strength and courage with gentleness, tenderness, and great unselfishness.[10]

THEODORE ROOSEVELT CAME BY his family values honestly—he gained them from his family, and in particular, his father. The way the great man deported himself in public and private—from the time he was a youngster to the time he was the best-known and best-loved man in America—was a determined effort to simply follow in the footsteps of his father.

Though he died when he was only forty-six, Roosevelt's father was a man of extraordinary character and accomplishment. A successful businessman, a tireless philanthropist, a determined patriot, a committed family man, a refined intellectual, a faithful Christian, and an energetic outdoorsman, he was everything that Roosevelt himself always strove to be.

According to journalist Jacob Riis, he was "a man of untiring energy, of prodigious industry, the most valiant fighter in his day for the right, and the winner of his fights."[11] Not surprisingly, his son would often sigh when, as governor or colonel or president, he had accomplished something for which his father had striven and paved the way, "Oh, how I wish Father were here and could see it."[12]

It was from his father that Roosevelt gained his great love of life: "He drove a four-in-hand in the park, sailed a boat, loved the woods, shared in every athletic sport, and was the life of every company,"[13] he remembered. But it was also from his father that he developed a sense of justice, righteousness, and discipline: "He would not tolerate in us children selfishness, cruelty, idleness, cowardice, or untruthfulness. With great love and patience and the most understanding and consideration, he combined insistence on discipline. He never physically punished me but once, but he was the only man of whom I was ever really afraid. I do not mean that it was a wrong fear, for he was entirely just, and we children adored him."[14]

Roosevelt was convinced that leadership could not exist in isolation. Leadership had to be modeled after some tangible, practical, and realizable ideal. Thus all great leaders were, in truth, simply students of men of unimpeachable character, unreproachable courage, and unswerving vision. Leaders had mentors. They were disciples. Rather than striking out as lonely pioneers, they were willing to stand on the shoulders of those who had gone before. They were men who comprehended the sober notion of legacy.

Thus he never attempted to escape from the shadow of his father. He never tried to establish an independent reputation for himself. Instead, he always felt that he was accountable to a kind of family trust and a national covenant. In his mind, he was essentially an heir, not a progenitor:

We have been entrusted with much—each and every one of us. We have a glorious inheritance that we must honor. I have a special sense of that great legacy, being the son of the finest man, the happiest man, I have ever known. He showed me what it means to live for right. He was a living illustration of the American ideal and spirit. All that I have ever done has been little more than an attempt to live up to and honor that legacy.[15]

Undoubtedly, it was this sense of legacy that animated Roosevelt's commitment to his own children and grandchildren. He wanted to make certain that all the benefits he had enjoyed—the special bequest of his father's legacy—would be enjoyed by them as well. He was conscious of the fact that a great responsibility of every generation of parents is not so much to exercise leadership but to pass on to their children the necessary principles and resources for leadership—and then leave the outcome to providence.

Jacob Riis believed that the son was "intent on making his life but a monument to the father."[16] But because of that "selfless obedience," his life instead "became, in the hands of God's good providence, a monument to the hopes and dreams of us all."[17]

Of such uncommon character is true leadership forged.

The Strenuous Life

*I am of course in a perfect whirl of work and have every
kind of worry and trouble—but that's what I am here for,
and down at bottom, I enjoy it after all.*[18]

ROOSEVELT'S PASSION FOR LIFE was infectious. Everything about him
tingled with zest and vitality. He approached every circumstance and
situation with consummate gusto and enthusiasm. What others believed were obstacles, he considered adventures. What others
thought of as setbacks, he viewed as challenges.

As a result, children loved him—he had a flair for the dramatic
and the heroic. And he lived in perpetual motion. Adults were often
struck utterly speechless in his presence—his energies were often in-
comprehensible and always irrepressible.

When he was president, he took visiting dignitaries on his point-
to-point "rambles and romps" through Rock Creek Park. Setting a
blistering pace, he would cut a beeline course climbing over, wading
through, cutting under, or swimming across whatever crossed his
path. Washington observers were always amused by the sight of the
great man charging ahead while his guests desperately struggled to
keep up.

Once while hiking and climbing in the Adirondacks, he had a Secret Service agent lower him with a rope around his ankles into a wide gorge so he could take a close-up photograph of a bird's nest. But when the agent tried to pull the president up the cliff, he was unable to manage. Impatient, Roosevelt called to the man, "Just cut the rope." Horrified, the agent refused—there was a thirty-foot drop between the president and the rushing water below. "Cut the rope," Roosevelt insisted. By this time the agent was panic-stricken—but he could think of nothing to do. At last, the president took matters into his own hands and cut the rope himself. He plunged into the icy waters below. Terrified, the agent scrambled down a trail to the bottom of the gorge to discover the president lying at the water's edge, half-conscious, cut, bruised, and soaked to the bone. The great man looked up at him, smiled a huge toothy grin, and said, "My, wasn't that just bully!"

Roosevelt had a boxing ring set up in the White House and often invited professional prizefighters to go a few rounds with him. He was an avid football fan—and eventually helped to establish the National Collegiate Athletic Association so that the sport could be regulated. And of course he went hunting and fishing every chance he could get.

And it was not only his pursuit of daring physical activity that astonished his more placid contemporaries—he seemed to work more, read more, think more, study more, talk more, and do more than any other living man. People simply could not believe how diverse were his interests and his accomplishments. Henry Cabot Lodge called him "a living tornado."[19] Henry Adams said he "crams more into a day than most men can hope to in a month."[20] And John Hay quipped, "I get tired just thinking about his schedule."[21]

In short, Theodore Roosevelt indulged in an unprecedented life of unceasing activity. And yet his intense ardor was not the result of mere hyperactivity. It was the carefully worked out result of his credo. It was the manifestation of his world view. It was the essence of his philosophy of life:

> I wish to preach not the doctrine of ignoble ease but the doctrine of the strenuous life; the life of toil and effort; of labor and strife; to preach that highest form of success which comes not to the man who desires mere easy peace but to the man who does not shrink from danger, hardship, or from the bitter toil, and who out of these wins the splendid ultimate triumph.[22]

Roosevelt did not believe greatness could be inherited. Our great legacy merely affords us with potential. It is up to each succeeding generation to give a good account of what they have been given. "Leaders are those," he asserted, "who make the most of every moment, of every opportunity, and of every available resource."[23]

To be sure, he practiced what he preached.

The Great Outdoors

I love all the seasons: the snows and bare woods of winter, the rush of growing things and the blossom spray of spring, the leafy shades that are heralded by the green dance of summer, and the sharp fall winds that tear the brilliant banners with which the trees greet the dying year.[24]

THEODORE ROOSEVELT LOVED THE mystery, the beauty, and the majesty of creation. Almost every aspect of his life—from the way he raised his children to the way he conducted his politics, from the way he spent his leisure time to the way he pursued his intellectual interests, from the way he related to other men to the way he invested his resources—revolved around his passion for the natural world.

He spent almost every minute he could outdoors. His enthusiastic involvement in hiking through the woods, riding horseback across the fields, hunting in the wilderness, rowing across lakes and bays—to say nothing of his climbing, sailing, swimming, trekking, picnicking, bird-watching, and gardening—was legendary. He was by all accounts "the greatest sportsman of his day."[25]

All of Roosevelt's most beautiful and eloquent writing—the foreword to *African Game Trails*, *A Booklover's Holidays in the Open*, and *The Wilderness Hunter*—vibrate to this note of a passionate love of nature. His letters are filled with observations from nature. His speeches make generous use of outdoor allusions and illustrations. His mind was utterly possessed by the glory of the created order.

John Burroughs, the great naturalist, declared that he did not know "any man with a keener and more comprehensive interest in nature and wild life—an interest both scientific and human."[26] Indeed, very few could even come close to matching his field skills, knowledge, or instincts.

Once, while visiting Yellowstone National Park, Roosevelt thought he heard the rather indistinct song of a Bullock's oriole. The scientists and naturalists accompanying the president assured him that he must be mistaken. Though such birds were known in the area, it was much too early—by a matter of months—for them to make an appearance. "Well, I am nearly certain that I caught a hint of two brief notes which could not be those of any other," he replied. Gently, the experts attempted to disabuse Roosevelt of the obviously mistaken notion. "Perhaps you have the song twisted," they suggested. But then, that evening as they were concluding their meal, the president suddenly laid down his fork, exclaiming, "Look! Look!" On a shrub outside the cabin window was a Bullock's oriole. The men were astonished. Roosevelt simply grinned and said, "Aha. Just as I suspected."[27]

One of the practical ends of his love of creation was the launching of a viable movement to protect and conserve America's natural resources. According to the *Encyclopedia Britannica*, "If Roosevelt did not invent the term conservation, he literally created as well as led the movement which made conservation one of the foremost political and social questions in the United States."[28] Certainly, the priority he placed on setting apart the great remaining wilderness areas, nature preserves, and wooded lands to be held in perpetuity as national parks and forests was one of the chief accomplishments of his administration. He believed it was incumbent upon every generation to ensure that succeeding generations would have the same opportunities to appreciate, enjoy, and benefit from the splendor of the nation's natural resources.

Even so, he would hardly have sympathized with modern environmentalism. As Edward Wagenknecht has argued, "He never sentimentalized nature or denied that it was red in tooth and claw."[29] His love of nature did not obscure his comprehension of its fallen estate and its ultimate subservience to the interests of man.

Leadership is the art of pursuing the ideal in the midst of a world that is less than ideal—and never losing sight of either notion. Thus the stewardship of nature was Roosevelt's chief concern, not the sanctity of nature. Such balance is rare indeed.

An Appetite for Learning

I am rather more apt to read old books than new ones.[30]

FRANCIS BACON ONCE MUSED, "Histories make men wise; poets, witty; mathematics, subtle; natural philosophy, deep; morals, grave; logic and rhetoric, able to contend."[31] Theodore Roosevelt took that counsel to heart. He was a voracious learner and an avid reader throughout his extraordinary life.

Among his friends he counted the greatest writers, thinkers, scholars, and scientists of his day. And by all accounts he was the best read of them all—being readily conversant on everything from the traditional classics to the most recent philosophical, sociological, or technological musings. He usually read at least five books a week—unless he wasn't too busy, in which case he read more. And yet his attitude toward the torrid pace of his intellectual pursuit was refreshingly relaxed:

> I am old-fashioned or sentimental, or something about books. Whenever I read one I want, in the first place, to enjoy myself, and, in the next place, to feel that I am a little better and not a little worse for having read it.[32]

His son Quentin claimed that his father read every book received at the Library of Congress—which of course he did not. But many of his friends testified that however new the volume they recommended to him, he had always read it already. "His range of reading is amazing," wrote the brilliant writer H. G. Wells. "He seems to be echoing with all the thought of the time, and he has receptivity to the pitch of genius."[33] Guglielmo Marconi, the great Italian physicist and inventor, was amazed by Roosevelt's knowledge in the specialized field of Italian history and literature. "That man actually cited book after book that I've never heard of, much less read. He's going to keep me busy for some time just following his Italian reading."[34] English diplomat Lord Charnwood asserted, "No statesman for centuries has had his width of intellectual range."[35]

As a result of Roosevelt's relentless studies and his near perfect recall, his knowledge was highly integrated, and he was continually crossing boundaries, moving back and forth from one area of human knowledge to another. He was thus able to make connections that mere specialists were unable to make.

According to Viscount Lee, "Whether the subject of the moment was political economy, the Greek drama, tropical fauna or flora, the Irish sagas, protective coloration in nature, metaphysics, the technique of football, or post-futurist painting, he was equally at home with the experts and drew out the best that was in them."[36] Indeed, "In one afternoon," said his son Archie, "I have heard him speak to the foremost Bible student of the world, a prominent ornithologist, an Asian diplomat, and a French general, all of whom agreed that Father knew more about the subjects in which they had specialized than they did."

Indeed, his mind was omnivorous and his interests were dizzying. "Can you come for dinner either Wednesday or Friday?" he wrote to Henry Cabot Lodge's wife. Then we could discuss the Hittite Empire, the Pithecanthropus, Magyar love songs, the exact relations of the Atli of the *Volsunga Saga* to the Etzel of the *Nibelungenlied*, and both to Attila—with interludes about the rate bill, [Albert] Beveridge, and other matters of more vivid contemporary interest."

But for all his prodigious knowledge, he was supremely unpretentious. All he ever claimed for himself was zest, "delight in the play of the mind for its own sake."[37] But others were rather more impressed. Famed academic Vilhjalmur Stefansson asserted, "It is to be supposed, seeing that Roosevelt is human, that there must be some fields in which he is ill-informed, but none of these have ever come to my attention, nor, so far as I know, to the attention of any of my friends in the various spheres of scientific or cultural exploration."[38]

"If you want to lead, you must read," was a maxim that Roosevelt took seriously.[39] It was merely an extension of his philosophy of life: making the most of his mind was of a piece with making the most of his body. It was merely an exercise of good stewardship.

And exercise it he did.

Storyteller

I am in the mood for a good story. Of course, I am always in the mood for a good story.[40]

ROOSEVELT HAD ALL THE gifts and inclinations of a born storyteller. Not only did he have a vivid imagination, an insatiable curiosity, a rich classical education, a profound grasp of history, and an elephantine memory, he loved sharing his many enthusiasms with others. He loved to talk. And his gregarious personality seemed to naturally animate whatever he talked about.

Of all that he accomplished throughout the crowded hours of his life, storytelling was among his favorite occupations. In fact, he wove storytelling into all of his other activities as best he could. His speeches were filled with vignettes from history. His conversations regularly recounted heroic incidents and episodes from the past. His correspondence was well seasoned with the lessons of yore. His favorite time of day was when he would gather his children around him for a bedtime story each evening. For years he taught a boys' Sunday school class—primarily because he so loved telling and retelling the stories of the Bible.

His friends testified that he was a dominating conversationalist—and that could be rather intimidating at times. He was always more than a little rambunctious, especially when he became enthralled with the course of a discussion—he was an incorrigible table thumper, conversation interrupter, and backslapper. Richard Watson Gilder noted he was "a human volcano, roaring as only a human volcano can roar—leading the laughing and the singing and the shouting, like a boy out of school, pounding the table with both noisy fists."[41] Gamaliel Bradford quipped, "He killed mosquitoes as if they were lions and lions as if they were mosquitoes."[42] Everyone around him was either utterly captivated and enthralled or entirely exhausted and cowed. But either way, they all agreed, Roosevelt had a knack for rich and compelling prose—often pouring forth in an unending stream.

Of course, his storytelling prowess was not limited to his speeches, monologues, and conversations. From his earliest youth to full maturity, Roosevelt wrote furiously on everything that interested him. Indeed, there were long stretches of his life when writing provided his principal income.

According to Mark Twain, if Theodore Roosevelt had not gone into politics, "he might have completely dominated America's literary scene."[43] Robert Frost asserted that Roosevelt had the "innate ability to craft sterling prose and gripping narrative."[44] Julian Street observed, "Roosevelt was a congenital writer and story-teller."[45] And Henry Cabot Lodge claimed that Roosevelt possessed "a rare and instinctive grasp of the art of narrative prose—he could have excelled as a journalist, an historian, a novelist, or a playwright."[46] As it was, Roosevelt somehow wrote almost sixty books during his mind-bogglingly busy career—books of stunning variety—ranging from biographies and histories to natural science and current political controversy.

Several of the books are acknowledged classics in their fields. *The Naval War of 1812*—which was hardly more than the work of a boy—remains a required text at naval academies on both sides of the Atlantic. *The Winning of the West* is placed alongside the histories of Francis Parkman as among the best of its kind. *Hunting Trips of a Ranchman, Ranch Life and the Hunting Trail,* and *The Wilderness Hunter* created an entirely new genre and spawned interest in the "wild, wild West." His profiles of Thomas Hart Benton, Gouverneur Morris, and Oliver Cromwell continue to serve as correctives to the smothering dominance of academic scientism in modern historical and biographical studies. And his controversial tomes—*Realizable Goals, Fear God and Take Your Own Part,* and *The Foes of Our Own Household*—ring more prophetically true today than even in his own day.

Despite his great prolificacy and his obvious inclinations toward the storytelling art, Roosevelt never took his gift for granted. Nor did he find the task of committing his thoughts to words carefree and effortless:

> Writing is horribly hard work to me; and I make slow progress. My style is very rough and I do not like a certain lack of sequitur that I do not seem to be able to get out of it.[47]

Nevertheless, he saw the proclamation of his essential principles as a vital aspect of his calling. He did not believe that he could lead the nation if he could not vividly portray the path down which he wished to take it. Indeed, "Where there is no vision, the people perish."[48] And so, until he took his final breath, he was a compelling and compulsive storyteller.

Good Deeds

I have a horror of words that are not translated into deeds, of speech that does not result in action.[49]

ACCORDING TO SHAKESPEARE, "Talkers are no good doers."[50] But there can be little doubt that Theodore Roosevelt violated that rule; though a talker, he was also a remarkable good doer.

The offices he held, the movements he led, the reforms he ensured, the feats he achieved, and the accomplishments that he attained seemed to have been enough for a dozen lifetimes. But for him, there were always new vistas, new hazards, and new demands that drove him onward.

Perhaps the greatest of these challenges was the recovery of American life and culture from the fanatical fringe. According to biographer Edward Wagenknecht, "He was of the stuff of which martyrs are made, yet he had none of the fanaticism commonly associated with martyrs."[51] He was not extremist enough for most of his critics but had a tireless gift for compromise and adjustment. Indeed, he had what he called "a Greek horror of extremes."[52] As Henry Cabot Lodge said of him:

He held to the golden middle course, not tepidly or timorously, but with the zeal and conviction of a crusader. He was a middle-of-the-road man, not because he was unwilling or afraid of committing himself to the position on either side, but he found the way to truth to lie midway between the two extremes. He was a zealot and fighter for truth, justice, and righteousness. He found no monopoly of any one of these precious possessions in the camp of extremists on either side. He found moderation the one virtue everyone wished to ignore.[53]

And so he became a champion of the ordinary concern. He became a spokesman for the common man. He became an advocate for the everyday affair. He did so because he was gripped by the truth of Edmund Burke's famous truism, "The only thing necessary for the triumph of evil is for good men to do nothing."[54]

He entered politics because he saw a need—not because he saw an opportunity. He plunged into every great task—reforming the civil service, blocking the manipulations of the political machines, restructuring the criminal justice system, reinvigorating the military establishment, and reinventing the political campaign—because of a sense of calling and a sense of duty to simply do what was right:

The foes of our own household are our worst enemies; and we can oppose them, not only by exposing them and denouncing them, but by constructive work in planning and building reforms which shall take into account both the economic and the moral factors in human advance.[55]

He had nothing but contempt for those who knew what was right but failed to act. He could not stand the idea that people might suggest a course of action for others that they themselves were not willing to take. He himself was an undoubted intellectual, but he reserved only enmity for the indolence of the ivory tower.

He read Cotton Mather's famous monograph *To Do Good* at least a dozen times—more than any other book besides Walter Scott's *Waverley* and John Bunyan's *Pilgrim's Progress*. That great colonial Puritan credo became his moral beacon light. He believed that the future of American civilization fully depended upon faithful men translating their good intentions into good deeds:

> We in America can attain our great destiny only by service; not by rhetoric, and above all not by insincere rhetoric, and that dreadful mental double-dealing and verbal juggling which makes promises and repudiates them, and says one thing at one time, and the directly opposite thing at another time. Our service must be the service of deeds.[56]

To his mind, true leadership was the ability to model for the people a pattern of behavior that was not content to deal in mere purposes and intentions. For him, true leadership was always intent on exposing the hypocrisy of believing one thing and doing another. True leadership was a life committed to good deeds.

Reformer

I believe in waging relentless war on rank-growing evils of all kinds.[57]

THE ROLE OF THE reformer is one of the most difficult and dangerous in all of civic life—especially if the reformer resists the urge to embrace all extremes and holds to the conservative course of balance and moderation. Theodore Roosevelt discovered this hard truth early on in his political career:

> It is not always easy to keep the just middle, especially when it happens that on one side are corrupt and unscrupulous demagogues, and on the other side corrupt and unscrupulous reactionaries.[58]

During his first term as a state legislator in New York, he ran into trouble with the political bosses almost immediately upon arriving in Albany. On the floor of the assembly he had issued a clarion call for an investigation into the corrupt judicial and civil service systems—much to the dismay of those whose vested interests might be threatened by such an investigation. They decided to teach him a lesson. One night as he was leaving a hotel buffet where legislators met after hours to discuss various issues, he was confronted by a noisy crowd of well-to-do businessmen and raconteurs. Among them was an infamous boxer named "Stubby" Collins. The pugilist proceeded to jostle Roosevelt with some force—and with a great show of indignation, demanded that the young legislator apologize for "running into him." But then, without waiting for his reply, Collins took a swipe at him. Roosevelt, now realizing that the throng of businessmen had hired the thug to beat him up, prepared to defend himself. The fight lasted less than a minute. Collins had more than met his match. As several astonished bystanders helped the badly beaten boxer off the floor, Roosevelt walked across the lobby and pleasantly informed the promoters of the affair that he understood their connection with it and was greatly obliged to them. "I have not enjoyed anything so much for a year," he said. And with that, he made his way out into the night.

With such pluck and aplomb, Roosevelt always faced his opposition. He did not expect his reforms to be received without the howls and groans of political conflict. Nevertheless he never shied away from a fight. "Right is right and wrong is wrong, " he asserted. "Woe be unto the man who shies away from the battle for justice and righteousness simply because the minions of injustice and unrighteousness are arrayed against him."[59]

And so, throughout his career Roosevelt was forever sticking his nose into affairs that more cautious politicians had always done their utmost to leave alone—labor relations, tax reform, racial reconciliation, conservationism, monopolization, civil rights, eugenics, segregation, abortion, bureaucratic inefficiency, and judicial corruption. For him, it was simply a matter of calling.

But for a man who was so driven by a sense of justice and righteousness, he was surprisingly practical. He understood how the game of politics worked. He was not adverse to the give and take of political negotiation. He knew the value of the art of compromise and he practiced it—as long as his compromises never diminished his principles. He was a coalition builder. He kept his eye on the prize, and was not overly concerned with the proprieties of party or partisanship as long as good ends were attained:

> The important thing generally is the next step. We ought not to take it unless we are sure that it is advisable; but we should not hesitate to take it once we are sure; and we can safely join with others who also wish to take it, without bothering our heads overmuch as to any somewhat fantastic theories that they may have concerning, say, the two hundredth step, which is not yet in sight.[60]

This approach generally drove his opponents mad—partly because it was so successful, and partly because it was so unpredictable. But for Roosevelt such an approach was the very essence of leadership. His goal, first and foremost, was to reach the goal.

Socialism

It is difficult to make our material condition better by the best of laws, but it is easy enough to ruin it by bad laws.[61]

THEODORE ROOSEVELT WAS NO friend of the great accumulators of wealth who dominated the worlds of politics, industry, and commerce in his day. From the beginning of his career, he confronted men like Jay Gould, J. P. Morgan, John D. Rockefeller, and Andrew Carnegie. He spearheaded a determined enforcement of the Sherman Antitrust Act to break the stranglehold of gargantuan monopolies and trusts on the American economy—thus earning the moniker "the Trust Buster."[62]

Despite this, he was hardly a liberal—much less a socialist—in his economic views. He even wrote a book, entitled *The Foes of Our Own Household*, denouncing the whole concept of overly intrusive government interventionism in the daily affairs of life.

Essentially, he was simply determined to protect ordinary Americans against the "creeping dehumanization" of an ideological secularism that he believed was already beginning to dominate the national life.[63] Roosevelt believed it necessary to "employ a certain skepticism"[64] even at the expense of the "cult" of science—which all too often looked rather innocent and disinterested, but which was actually neither. Of course, he was not at all resistant to science or technological progress—in fact he took great glee in such. Instead, he was resistant to the crass and inhuman humanism that often accompanied the "industrial collectivization" of the "malefactors of great wealth."[65] He believed that any way of life that "omits or de-emphasizes either the freedom or the responsibility of individuals and families [was] necessarily disastrous to all dimensions of life and culture."[66]

As a result, he regarded socialism as well as monopolism, democratic liberalism as well as communism, and republican cooperationism as well as nationalistic fascism with equal disdain.[67] In fact, he professed an "ingrained suspicion" of all schemes that "proposed to coerce ordinary people" to their "alleged benefit."[68] He was, at heart, opposed to all manner of utopianism—whether of the Left or the Right.

Affected by the thinking of the Distributists of Britain, the Christian Democrats of Holland, and the early agrarians of the South, Roosevelt took a position that essentially affirmed the principles of free enterprise, small business ownership, and open fair trade without embracing the corporatism, mercantilism, and uniformitarianism of monopolistic capitalism. He feared that with the growth of American economic dependency on the huge industrial combines, most men and women were being reduced to a new kind of modern servile status—what he called "industrial serfs."

What he advocated as an alternative was a proliferation of new small business and property ownership. He did not want Americans to become the unpropertied wards of a huge messianic entity—be it the government or the corporation:

We are steadily bent on preserving the institution of private property; we combat every tendency toward reducing the people to economic servitude; and we care not whether the tendency is due to a sinister agitation directed against all property, or whether it is due to the actions of those members of the predatory classes whose anti-social power is immeasurably increased because of the very fact that they possess wealth.[69]

Nevertheless, he had little confidence in the agency of government to adequately address his concerns about consolidation. He was no starry-eyed liberal whose reform mantra was little more than "there ought to be a law." Instead, he remained more than a little suspicious of both the efficacy and the motivation of government social or economic programs. Indeed, were he to choose one or the other, he would always choose the private sector over the public as the best guarantor of freedom:

Under government ownership corruption can flourish just as rankly as under private ownership. I do not believe in government ownership of anything which can with propriety be left in private hands.[70]

Roosevelt was an idealist—but he was also blessed with a strong dose of realism. He knew that there were no simple or easy solutions to the grave problems that faced America and the world. As a result, he was the rarest of all politicians: he distrusted the ultimate efficacy of idealistic and ideological politics.

The Bully Pulpit

The White House is a bully pulpit.[71]

UPON LEAVING THE White House, Roosevelt declined an offer to sit on the board of a large corporation at a salary of $100,000 a year—an enormous amount of money at the time. Instead he accepted the position of associate editor of *Outlook* magazine—a small but highly regarded journal of cultural and political thought—at a salary of $12,000 a year. He told friends that he chose the better job. "I am far more interested in the influence I might be able to wield," he said, "speaking my heart and mind to the nation than I am in money or power."[72]

Throughout his life he considered his greatest contributions to American life to be those times when he spoke directly to the people. He was committed to politics and to the processes of government. But he knew only too well the grave limitations that the system imposed on real and substantive change. On the other hand, he had supreme confidence in the people to make wise decisions and to take appropriate actions—if only they were given the right information and the right opportunities.

Thus he was vigilant in his efforts to communicate. He was the first president to effectively use the press to his own political advantage. Every other chief executive only had tolerated journalists and photographers. Roosevelt embraced them. He gave them two short briefings every day. He kept them informed of his meetings, agendas, and policies. He made them an integral part of his overall political strategy.

In addition, Roosevelt was the first president to travel extensively to every section of the country. In his first administration alone, he made thirty-five trips outside of Washington—including an extensive tour of the South and a forty-five-thousand-mile journey from coast to coast. At every whistle-stop, at every historical site, at every major city, and at every scenic locale along the way, he mingled with the people, made speeches, and honored local dignitaries. He always did research on the local traditions, distinctives, and customs and then mentioned such in his speeches. In so doing, he not only wove an intricate grass-roots web of personal support, he put his stamp on the local consciousness. He earned the right to speak into their lives—because he came to them not as an outsider but as a compatriot.

He was born in the Northeast—and so had a natural affinity with the people there. But he made his name in the West—so the people in that region claimed him as his own. His maternal family line was one of the most distinguished in the old South—and he made good use of those connections as well. Indeed, he could lay claim to being the first president whose support entirely transcended regionalism and parochialism. And he unashamedly used that tremendous advantage to advance his various political causes and positions.

All of this was a part of Roosevelt's determined strategy to use the White House as a "bully pulpit." It was his very deliberate attempt to bypass the gridlock of politics as usual and instead take his message directly to the people.

Because he believed that the role of the leader was primarily to serve as a moral compass—pointing the nation toward the true north of justice and righteousness—he took every opportunity to inform the people, to encourage them, to exhort them, to reprove them, to stimulate them, and to inspire them. He dedicated every high school, opened every bridge, presided at every anniversary, visited every monument, and convened every convention he possibly could. His pulpit was employed with an evangelist's fervor:

> We must diligently strive to make our young men decent, God-fearing, law-abiding, honor-loving, justice-doing, and also fearless and strong, able to hold their own in the hurly-burly of the world's work, able to strive mightily that the forces of right may be in the end triumphant. And we must be ever vigilant in so telling them.[73]

His presidential addresses and speeches alone would eventually comprise seven thick volumes—a prodigious output, especially considering the fact that he used no speech writers. But Roosevelt believed that such herculean labors were an essential component of his leadership task:

> The man who knows the truth and has the opportunity to tell it, but who nonetheless refuses to, is among the most shameful of all creatures. God forbid that we should ever become so lax as that.[74]

The Common Man

*The nameless pioneers and settlers, the obscure mothers
and fathers, the quiet craftsmen and tradesmen; it is
only among these that the real story of America is told;
it is only among them that the brilliance of liberty may
be comprehended.*[75]

IN HIS BOOK *Hero Tales from American History*, Theodore Roosevelt
chose to profile a number of little-known individuals and incidents.
It was in the ordinary conduct of ordinary lives in ordinary circumstances that he believed "the genius of the American civilization"
was most effectively made known.[76]

He believed that it was a noble pursuit to remind people—especially, to remind young people—of the men and women of the past
"who showed that they knew how to live and how to die; who
proved their truth by their endeavor."[77] And more often than not,
the best exemplars of such heroic virtue were not the famous or the
prominent but the forgotten and the obscure.

And so he gave much of his life to helping people to remember, cherish, and protect the glorious accomplishments of the common man.

G. K. Chesterton—one of Roosevelt's favorite contemporary
writers—often asserted, "The most extraordinary thing in the world

is an ordinary man and an ordinary woman and their ordinary children."[78] Ultimately that is one of the great lessons of history. It is that ordinary people are the ones who determine the outcome of human events in the end—not kings and princes, not masters and tyrants. It is laborers and workmen, cousins and acquaintances that upend the expectations of the brilliant and the glamorous, the expert and the meticulous. It is plain folks, simple people, who literally change the course of history—because they are the stuff of which history is made. They are the ones who make the world go round.

In his years on the western range, during his battles to reform the civil service system and the police department, on the field of battle with the Rough Riders, and throughout his many campaigns, Roosevelt had come to have a deep and abiding admiration for the workaday citizens who faithfully tended their gardens, raised their children, perfected their trades, and minded their businesses. He had become utterly convinced that in America the heroic could be found more readily in the mundane than in the profane, that glory might be discovered more obviously in commonness than in prominence, and that the least and the last were, in truth, the first and the foremost.

Jacob Riis claimed that by championing this peculiarly unmodern conception in both politics and life, Roosevelt has left an extraordinary cultural legacy to the nation he loved so dearly:

> He knew well the importance of history, of remembering the great and mighty deeds of the past. But he knew equally well the importance of remembering what was actually important in history; of discerning what were in truth the great and mighty deeds; of retaining that which may be neglected by the text books, but must never be by the ordinary citizen. He therefore unashamedly staked his claim with the common man.[79]

As a result of this remarkable conviction, he consciously chose to rearrange his priorities so his daily schedule might better reflect his true principles—even when that proved to be a source of profound irritation to the rich, famous, and powerful men around him.

For instance, he often postponed serious affairs of state in order to converse with average citizens. Once he left two senators, five congressmen, and the heads of seven major corporations to wait in the White House for two hours while he discussed flora and fauna with a half dozen truck farmers from Alabama. When he finally showed the influential men into his office, one of the senators sternly rebuked him, "Mr. President, you must stand by your priorities." To which Roosevelt responded, "Oh, but I did, Senator. I did."

On another occasion, he slipped out of a very dull but apparently important diplomatic reception at the German Embassy to watch the last few innings of a baseball game. When the White House press corps caught up with him, they asked if he was not concerned that his actions might cause the German Empire to take offense. He replied, "I'm more concerned that this local nine might take offense—since I missed the first five innings of their championship match."[80]

Roosevelt knew that what was really important in life rarely put on airs of importance. And ultimately, he believed that this was the surest test of true leadership in a free republic.

Humility

I am just an ordinary man, without any special ability in any direction.[81]

DESPITE HIS PRODIGIOUS LEARNING, his prolific accomplishments, and his popular fame, Roosevelt remained unaffected. Throughout his life he was forthrightly modest. Though he was the most dominating public figure of his time, he consistently maintained that he was not a great man:

> In most things I am just about average; in some of them a little under, rather than over. I am only an ordinary walker. I can't run. I am not a good swimmer, although I am a strong one. I probably ride better than anything else I do, but I am certainly not a remarkably good rider. I am not a good shot. I never could be a good boxer, although I do keep at it, whenever I can. My eyesight prevents me from ever being a good tennis player, even if otherwise I could qualify. I am not a brilliant writer. I have written a great deal, but I always have to work and slave over everything I write. The things I have done are all, with the possible exception of the Panama Canal, just such things as any ordinary man

could have done. There is nothing brilliant or outstanding in my record at all.[82]

This was not false modesty. Nor was it self-disparagement. It was, he believed, instead a genuine and honest assessment of his abilities. When he compared himself to the great men of the past—his own heroes from American history—he always felt he came up lacking.

Roosevelt consciously and consistently sought to apply the virtue of humility in his life. He tried to see himself in the light of truth. He carefully practiced the Christian principle of self-examination.

For example, often before retiring to bed, Roosevelt and his friend the naturalist William Beebe would step outside the White House and look up into the night sky, searching for a tiny patch of light near the constellation Pegasus. "That is the Spiral Galaxy in Andromeda," they would chant in unison. "It is as large as our Milky Way. It is one of a hundred million galaxies. It consists of one hundred billion suns, each larger than our own sun." After a moment of silent awe, Roosevelt would then turn to his companion and say, "Now I think we are small enough. Let's go to bed."[83]

Roosevelt was quite impatient with the sycophants who cluttered his private life and fawned over him in public. "I don't care a rap for popularity," he would often quip.[84] And he was utterly indifferent to presidential protocol. He could never get used to being served first at meals in the White House, and he violently objected to ladies rising in his presence. After all, he believed that the commonplace things of ordinary mannerliness and human relations took precedence over all issues of office or position.

His sense of what was truly impressive in life also greatly contributed to his stunning humility:

There are two kinds of success. One is the very rare kind that comes to the man who has the power to do what no one else has the power to do. That is genius. Whether it is the genius of the man who can write a poem that no one else can write, The Ode on a Grecian Urn, for example, or Helen, Thy Beauty Is to Me; or of a man who can do one hundred yards in nine and three-fifths seconds; only a very limited amount of the success of life comes to persons possessing genius. The average man who is successful—the average statesman, the average public servant, the average soldier, who wins what we call success—is not a genius. He is a man who has merely the ordinary qualities that he shares with his fellows, but who has developed those ordinary qualities to a more than ordinary degree.[85]

There can be little doubt that Roosevelt would have preferred to be known in history as an average man rather than a genius. He would have much rather been known as a man who developed his ordinary qualities to a more than ordinary degree. His motto was simply, "Do what you can, with what you've got, where you are."[86]

There is little extraordinary about the achievements of a genius, a prodigy, or a savant. Inevitably, a great leader is someone who overcomes tremendous obstacles and still succeeds. Thus did Theodore Roosevelt succeed—overcoming a sickly childhood, personal tragedy, and fierce opposition from the vested interests—to lead the world with unmatched vision and valor.

His son Kermit truthfully could confess, "Father had no sense of his own greatness, only of the greatness of opportunity that each of us has."[87]

War and Peace

A just war is in the long run far better for a man's soul than the most prosperous peace.[88]

CRITICS OF THEODORE ROOSEVELT often found it difficult to oppose a man of such immense popularity, unbounded energy, and unmatched competency. He was practically immune to the ordinary discourse of political contention. The only tactic with which they found consistent success was to accuse him of reckless impetuousness, ambitious adventurism, and hotheaded warmongering in the all too delicate area of international affairs.

To be sure, Roosevelt was plainspoken in his pronouncements about the advantages of war and the dangers of peace in certain circumstances: "The things that will destroy America are prosperity-at-any-price, peace-at-any-price, safety-first instead of duty-first, the love of soft living, and the get-rich-quick theory of life."[89]

Though he had seen the horrors of war firsthand, he maintained a romantic image of its manly rectitude: "No qualities called out by a purely peaceful life stand on a level with those stern and virile virtues which move the men of stout heart and strong hand who uphold the honor of their flag in battle."[90]

Indeed, he felt that a willingness to go to war for a just cause was a kind of litmus test of its integrity and honor: "A nation is not wholly admirable unless in times of stress it will go to war for a great ideal."[91]

Conversely, his view of peace—particularly the sort of peace at any price that many isolationists advocated—was all too often a misnomer for something less than a shameful betrayal of all that the American experiment in liberty stood for:

> Peace is generally good in itself, but it is never the highest good unless it comes as the handmaiden of righteousness; and it becomes a very evil thing if it serves merely as a mask for cowardice and sloth, or as an instrument to further the ends of despotism or anarchy.[92]

Quite naturally, many men and women across the country feared that once he attained the office of the presidency, the nation would be perpetually mired in one misbegotten military adventure after another. But of course, that simply was not the case. In fact, the two Roosevelt administrations were among the most peaceful and harmonious in all of American history. And as if that were not enough, the president was awarded the Nobel Peace Prize for his role in negotiating the end to the bitter Russo-Japanese War in 1905—the first American so honored.

A reporter once asked Roosevelt about this paradox. He kiddingly replied, "I certainly would never have started a war I couldn't have fought in."[93] In truth, Roosevelt's military policy was designed to enforce peace through strength: "I only advocate preparation for war in order to avert war; and I should never advocate war itself unless it were the only possible alternative to shame and dishonor."[94]

In 1908 he commissioned a complete American battle fleet under the command of Adm. Robert Evans to circle the globe. The ships were painted a brilliant white for their forty-two-thousand-mile show of force. Though critics were appalled at such blatant saber rattling, Roosevelt contended that the famed "Great White Fleet" had "exercised a greater influence for peace than all the peace conferences of the last fifty years."[95]

He believed that the essence of leadership was the ability to maintain great strength without any impulsive compulsion to use it. That strength was to be held in reserve until, and unless, it became necessary to use it for the cause of right:

> I abhor unjust war. I abhor injustice and bullying by the strong at the expense of the weak, whether among nations or individuals. I abhor violence and bloodshed. But it takes strength to put a stop to abhorrent things.[96]

And so the peace was kept.

Science

The tracing of an unbroken line of descent from the protozoan to Plato does not in any way really explain Plato's consciousness.[97]

THEODORE ROOSEVELT THOUGHT OF himself as a man of science. From childhood he immersed himself in the accouterments and the ethos of a scientific life. Until his final year in college he was planning to dedicate his full concerns to scientific pursuits. Even after he launched into the career trajectory of politics and journalism, he maintained a lively interest and an active hand in scientific matters.

And his involvement was hardly amateurish. Academicians, naturalists, and scientific specialists were continually astonished at the depth of his insight and understanding. The great ornithologist Frank Chapman claimed, "The President knows more about birds than I do."[98] South American zoologist Ferdinand Zahm was amazed "by his broad and exact knowledge of the flora and fauna of lands he had never yet visited."[99] And scientific historian C. Hart Merriam called him "the world's authority on the big game mammals of North America."[100]

The Natural History Museum at the Smithsonian Institution once had a specimen of a prematurely born mammal that no one on the prestigious staff could identify. So they sent the specimen to the White House. Roosevelt not only identified it at once but supplied the scientists with a tremendous amount of information that greatly expedited their researches.

On another occasion he visited a laboratory at the museum where some five thousand skulls, in various stages of disarray, were being assembled by a crack team of experts. Roosevelt astonished everyone—including several eminent naturalists who were visiting the site—by picking up skull after skull and mentioning the scientific name of the genus to which each belonged.

On yet another occasion a paleontologist mentioned to him a very obscure species of mouse that had recently been discovered in a remote section of northern British Columbia. He supposed that none but a very well-informed specialist would know anything about the rodent. But upon mention of it, Roosevelt immediately began to tell him all about it. He was perfectly familiar with the little animal.

But despite his minute familiarity with the natural sciences, he was not prone—as so many scientists are—to the fads and fancies of scientific inquiry. He did not believe that simply because technology made a thing possible, it should necessarily be done. He did not accept the notion of unfettered progress simply for the sake of progress:

> Progress has brought us both unbounded opportunities and unbridled difficulties. Thus, the measure of our civilization will not be that we have done much, but what we have done with that much. I believe that the next half century will determine if we will advance the cause of Christian civilization or revert to the horrors of brutal paganism.[101]

The proper use of scientific knowledge and advancement was a supremely moral concern for him:

The thought of modern industry in the hands of Christian charity is a dream worth dreaming. The thought of industry in the hands of paganism is a nightmare beyond imagining. The choice between the two is upon us.[102]

Additionally, he was not susceptible to the smothering uniformity of scientific theorizing. Though he was comfortable with certain aspects of evolutionary theory, he was an outspoken critic of Darwinism—delivering several important papers challenging the unquestioning faith of many scientists in the theory. When he delivered the Romanes Lectures at Oxford University, he highlighted "the fallacy of using parallels between the evolution of animal life and the development of human societies and glib attempts to apply Darwinism to social development."[103]

He believed that science—like politics—was merely a tool or a resource to be used for the good of mankind—not an end unto itself. And its limitations and inadequacies were always to be kept in full view.

He believed that a wise leader always uses whatever resources are placed at his disposal—but he never confused the means with the ends.

The South

I can quite legitimately claim to be a proud son of the South.[104]

THE WOUNDS OF THE War Between the States were still aching and raw when Theodore Roosevelt arrived in the White House. It had only been twenty-five years since the end of Reconstruction, and the bitterness between North and South remained unabated. And although the Spanish-American War had had an enormous unifying effect on certain portions of both regions, the nation was still scarred by a great emotional, cultural, and economic divide.

Roosevelt was the first president to self-consciously cross that divide. His paternal relations were all Northern Unionists, through and through. But all his maternal relations were thoroughly unreconstructed Southerners. And so he was actually able to embrace the best of both traditions.

The Bulloch family of Roswell, Georgia, boasted a member of the Continental Congress, the first governor of Georgia, and a brigadier general in the Continental army. Their plantation home, Bulloch Hall, was one of the most magnificent in the South and the hub of the region's social, political, and cultural relations. Margaret Mitchell, who wrote about the house early in her career as an Atlanta newspaper reporter, used it as the model for Tara in her novel *Gone with the Wind*.[105]

Two of Roosevelt's Bulloch uncles served with distinction in the navy of the Confederate States of America. James Dunwoodie Bulloch, at the outbreak of hostilities between North and South, was a captain in the merchant marine. His ship was in port at New Orleans at the time of the secession of Louisiana from the Union, and the governor demanded the vessel be handed over to the state. Bulloch refused—he believed honor required him to deliver the vessel into the hands of her owners in New York. As soon as he had fulfilled his obligations, however, Bulloch presented himself to President Jefferson Davis for service to his country. He was immediately commissioned a captain in the fledgling navy. He became one of the most successful blockade-runners in the South. Later he was sent to England to buy and equip vessels of war. The British government was forbidden by the laws of neutrality to permit such a thing—but Captain Bulloch's ingenuity prevailed. He was eventually able to set sail at least a half dozen ships under the Confederate Stars and Bars—including the warship, CSS *Alabama*.

Irvine Stephens Bulloch, the captain's younger brother, became the navigating officer of the *Alabama*. When that great ship was finally sunk in a savage sea battle off the coast of France, the young Bulloch commanded the last gun that was in action and fired the last shot from her sinking deck. After the war, seeing their national cause utterly lost, both men chose to live out their lives in exile rather than submit to the humiliation of the devastating Reconstruction years.

Many of Theodore Roosevelt's fondest memories as a child were of visits to his two uncles in England. They regaled him with stories of the old South. They filled his mind with the sense of honor, filial duty, and undying valor that so marked the ideals of the Confederacy. And though he did not share their attachment to the doctrines of secession or servility, he never ceased to admire them and their legacy. He said that the two men "always struck me as the nearest approach to genuine heroes of any men I ever met in actual life."[106]

During his administration, Roosevelt made a point of including portions of the South as an integral part of every presidential tour. He visited Roswell, Georgia, nearly a dozen times—always asserting his affectionate attachment to the place. He completely altered the civil service system in the South—which had been by far the most corrupt in the nation since the time of Reconstruction—even to the point of appointing qualified Democrats rather than keeping the heirs of the carpetbaggers and scalawags on the federal dole. He often requested "Dixie"—which he considered "the best of all our national tunes"—to be played at various state dinners.[107]

By modern standards these may not seem to be particularly innovative measures. But at the turn of the century they were considered extraordinary reforms.

Roosevelt set out to unite the disparate and distinctive legacies of North and South in the same way they had been united in his own family. And in so doing, he helped the nation begin the vital process of healing—at long last.

Humor

THERE IS NOTHING IN a leader at once so sane and so sympathetic as a good sense of humor. That Theodore Roosevelt was possessed of prodigious jocularity, there can be little doubt

According to Henry Cabot Lodge, "No man ever had a more abundant sense of humor—joyous, irrepressible humor—and it never deserted him. Even at the most serious and perilous moments if there was a gleam of humor anywhere, he saw it and rejoiced and helped himself with it over the rough places and in the dark hour."[108]

He loved fun. He loved to joke. And he loved silly pranks. As Lodge recalled, "His ready smile and contagious laugh made count-less friends and saved him from many an enmity."[109]

Perhaps best of all, Roosevelt could laugh at himself—and there was plenty to laugh at. Because of his furious activity, he was constantly injuring himself. He obviously was not a clumsy man, and yet throughout his life he broke at least nineteen bones. And he endured more cuts, scrapes, bruises, and injuries than can be imagined, much less be counted. He dislocated a knee while chasing the children down the White House stairs. He suffered a concussion during a contraband football match in the Blue Room. And he was blinded in one eye during a boxing match with the former heavyweight champion of the world in the new executive office wing. Roosevelt saw the absurdity in this—and was often the first to burst out into laughter following one of his mishaps.

In addition, though, he had the ability to laugh right along with his political critics at his foibles, faux pas, and failures. He always enjoyed political cartoons—even when the joke came at his expense. And though he was scathing in his denunciations of yellow journalism, he never failed to appreciate the humor in political satire.

When people met him for the first time, invariably they would be impressed by his ready laugh and ear-to-ear grin. He had a very personable way of breaking down barriers and inhibitions with his infectious good humor. A fierce political opponent observed, "The problem with meeting with Roosevelt face to face is that you have to go in hating him an awful lot not to come out liking him even more."[110]

Wit was such an important part of his stump personae that several newspapers around the country began running a weekly column containing only jokes and humorous anecdotes from his speeches. Famed humor writer Homer Davenport asserted:

Theodore Roosevelt is a humorist. In the multitude of his strenuousness this, the most human of his accomplishments, has apparently been overlooked. There is a similarity between his humor and Mark Twain's. If Roosevelt were on the vaudeville stage he would be a competitor of Harry Lauder. No one can sit through one of his speeches with a straight face. He can make a joke as fascinating as he can the story of a sunset on the plains of Egypt.[111]

According to Jacob Riis, this "comic genius was simply the result of a happy life."[112] He loved life. He had fun. And he never took himself or any of his accomplishments too terribly seriously.

During the most difficult days of the 1912 campaign, when he was forced to take on both major established parties with no real political organization, a meager budget, and a hodgepodge staff, his happy disposition and good humor is nearly all that kept the progressives afloat. His lighthearted attitude toward "Hudge" (Wilson) and "Pudge" (Taft) kept his frustrated and discouraged volunteers in stitches. One of those workers later recalled:

> Some may remember Roosevelt for his legislative accomplishments. Others for his literary feats. Still others for his moral courage. But I will always remember him for his ability to take any circumstance and see it through the lens of happy providence. He was, for me, living proof of the fact that laughter is indeed the best medicine.[113]

Courage

My success so far has only been won by absolute indifference to my future career.[114]

HOW CAN YOU DESCRIBE the courage of Theodore Roosevelt other than to simply say it was inexhaustible. The instances of his physical and moral valor are almost too numerous to mention.

His experiences on the western range would be enough to rank him among the nation's most courageous men. He not only tamed the wilds of the frontier, he tamed the wild frontiersmen—capturing fugitives, domesticating renegades, and besting ruffians. In Africa he calmly dropped a rhinoceros in full charge at fifty paces. Once he killed a mountain lion while he was hanging over a cliff, head downward, with his guide holding on to his feet.

In battle Roosevelt was utterly fearless—charging up San Juan Hill under a withering fire from entrenched enemy positions. Years later when he had become commander in chief, he never asked his men to do anything he was not willing to do himself. And so he went up in a box-kite airplane, went down in a primitive submarine, flew in a zeppelin, and drove in an overland half-track.

He took his duty as president as a kind of pastoral charge. Before the day of presidential helicopters and jets, he visited the sites of disasters, storms, fires, and floods to comfort and encourage the victims. "I am going to New Orleans," he once wrote to his son Kermit during a particularly dire epidemic. "I believe the danger is infinitesimal, and I do not think a President ought ever, by his action, to give any chance to timid people to use his example as an excuse for their timidity."[115]

But as great as his physical courage obviously was, his moral courage was even greater. When he took on New York's corrupt political bosses single-handedly at the very beginning of his career, his enemies ridiculed him as a kid-gloved reformer. When he criticized Wilson's wartime policies at the very end of his career, he was condemned as an old has-been embittered with sour grapes. Neither reaction caused him to swerve for an instant from the course he had determined was right and good and true.

Whenever he had something unpleasant to say, he always seemed to find a way to say it to the most unsympathetic audience—he stated his commitment to the gold standard in the heart of the pro-silver belt; he defended the rigid New York blue laws in a downtown saloon district; he publicly rebuked the governor of Arkansas, sitting on the platform next to him, because he had implicationally defended racist lynchings; he condemned the rebels against British rule in an address in Cairo, though he had been warned that he would be shot if he even brought up the issue; and he received his friend Booker T. Washington on a dais in Jackson, Mississippi.

Time after time, establishment political operatives attempted to warn him against such impolitic maneuvers. But he was resolute. Anything less than absolute forthrightness, he considered a cowardly accommodation to officeholding—which was the very negation of true statesmanship:

I do not believe that any man should ever attempt to make politics his only career. It is a dreadful misfortune for a man to grow to feel that his whole livelihood and whole happiness depend upon his staying in office. Such a feeling prevents him from being of real service to the people while in office and always puts him under the heaviest strain of pressure to barter his convictions for the sake of holding office.[116]

His boldness on the stump, then, was a kind of personal insurance against compromise. The efficacy of his leadership depended, he believed, on his incognizance of the negative consequences of doing right. According to his friend Owen Wister, "He was indifferent to the outcome of a battle so long as he knew that he was on the right side, had given his all-in-all, and had had a bully time in the process."[117]

Failure

There is no disgrace in a failure, only in a failure to try.[118]

THEODORE ROOSEVELT WAS NEVER afraid to fail. In fact, he often wore his failures as badges of honor. To him, the attempt, the effort, and the sheer pluck of involvement was what really mattered in the end:

> Far better it is to dare mighty things, to win glorious triumphs, even though checkered by failure, than to take rank with those poor spirits who neither enjoy much nor suffer much because they live in the gray twilight that knows neither victory nor defeat.[119]

Though he enjoyed many successes throughout his career, he had his share of failures. He never allowed failure to stymie his sense of responsibility and calling. He was often knocked down but never out.

In addition, he was eager to learn from his mistakes. Once when his administration had lost a strategic legislative battle on the floor of the Senate, he called each of the men who had led the opposition to the White House. Expecting an angry tirade or an hysterical harangue, the senators were surprised when Roosevelt anxiously gathered them around his desk and asked for their advice. "How could I have handled this bill better? What did I say or not say to cause you to oppose it? What should I do in the future to better advance my principles?"[120] The men were stunned. There was no recrimination. There were no lectures. There were no threats. Instead, they found in the president an eager learner—ready to accept the blame for his own shortcomings and then to try to move on and do better on another day. One of them later confessed, "I learned more about leadership and greatness in that one incident than in all my previous years in politics."[121]

Elihu Root, who served as Roosevelt's secretary of state, called him "the most advisable man I ever knew."[122] John Hay, who designed the "Open Door" policy with China following the Boxer Rebellion, often marveled at the "amiability and open-mindedness" with which Roosevelt accepted advice.[123] "If he was convinced of your sincerity," said the Progressive leader Albert Beveridge, "you could say anything to him you liked. You could even criticize him personally."[124] And the author and social reformer Herbert Croly remarked that he had "never met a man so eager to learn from his mistakes—or even so ready to admit them. It was as if he had no ego."[125]

Just a month after the defeat of the Progressive ticket in 1912, when others were still licking their wounds, he was already analyzing, critiquing, and planning. His son Kermit observed:

> There are no full stops for him, no final defeats, and no ultimate victories. It seems that he is able to absorb every act of providence—be it good or bad from a human perspective—as one more necessary lesson in life. He is always growing, always learning, and always striving to make a better showing next time around. Each failure is for him merely an incomplete task along the way toward an ultimate success.[126]

Roosevelt was not simply a hopeless romantic or an unrealistic optimist in this regard. Rather he was a man who was secure enough in his calling and purpose in life to remain undeterred by obstacles along the way—be they great or small. Again, Kermit explained:

> Some men have a strong sense of destiny. I cannot say that Father could ever fully identify such sentiments in his own experience. But I am quite certain that he knew what to work toward. Whether he ever actually attained to it was another matter altogether—and one of little concern to him.[127]

For Roosevelt, true leadership not only involved a strength of character that was unafraid to admit failure, was willing to learn from error, and was quick to accept wise counsel, it also involved a sense of calling that was able to integrate such virtues into life with real confidence. For him, failure was the backdoor to success.

Friendship

*It may be true that he travels farthest who travels alone;
but the goal thus reached is not worth reaching.*[128]

THEODORE ROOSEVELT WAS A man of enormous social skills. He had
a compelling personal charisma that naturally drew others to himself. He was affable, gregarious, charming, and gracious. John Cater
Rose once remarked, "He gave every man he had talked with for five
minutes the impression that he liked him very much."[129]

He was a fascinating conversationalist. He was so remarkably
well-informed that he could speak intelligently about almost any
subject at length. But he by no means dominated discussions. Indeed, he was an avid listener who often remained rather quiet in
large public settings. He had a knack for bringing out the best in others. Thus, according to Albert Schauffler:

> Though a brilliant, humorous, high-powered talker, he was more ear
> than mouth. On the slightest indication that another had anything to
> contribute, he would jam on all his verbal brakes. He was perhaps the

most creative listener I have ever encountered. If we all had such audiences, we would continually excel ourselves.[130]

He was a great encourager. He liked nothing better than to see others succeed. He marveled, even reveled, in the manifest gifts of others. And he was abundantly profusive in his praise of their achievements. As Irvin Cobb put it, "You had to hate Roosevelt a whole lot to keep from loving him."[131]

As a result, he was a great friend—and he attracted a great variety of intimates. From his schooldays at Harvard he maintained life-long friendships with such men of culture and refinement as William Roscoe Thayer, Harry Shaw, and Minot Weld. From his years in the West he maintained long-term relationships with rough-and-tumble cowboys like Bill Sewall, Will Dow, and Bill Merrifield. From the world of politics he gained the devotion of cunning strategists like Elihu Root, John Hay, and Henry Cabot Lodge. He was close to a number of scientists—John Muir, C. Hart Merriam, and William Beebe; military men—Fitzhugh Lee, Leonard Wood, George Dewey; and writers—Jacob Riis, Rudyard Kipling, and Owen Wister. All of them treasured his company and companionship as among the most significant in their lives.

He was loyal, compassionate, tender-hearted, and most of all, fun. He always remembered names, special occasions, and intimate details about conversations that made his friends feel a sense of supreme importance.

Amazingly though, Roosevelt was not a particularly social person. Though he dearly loved his friends, he always preferred a quiet night at home with Edith and the children to anything or anyone else. He did not enjoy going out. He was not a "joiner."[132] And he was convinced that he was a poor "mixer."[133] He hated parties and social occasions—especially if he knew that he was to be the center of attention, which he almost always was. "Huge banquets and such" were "horrid functions" in his eyes.[134] He always felt that he would be "caught" by some dominating boor or "button-holed" by some dim acquaintance—and often begged Edith to keep an eye out to "rescue him" if necessary.[135] For the more frivolous activities of organized society he felt only contempt. "My own family, good book, a roaring fire, and a simple meal on the porch, now that is my idea of a bully social event."[136] Both he and Edith loathed staying in other people's homes. When he was traveling he much preferred what he called "an old fogey hotel."[137] And his favorite restaurants were "often rather disreputable hole in the wall joints."[138]

He was, in reality, an intensely private person. He had only a handful of close friends with whom he shared his most intimate concerns. Henry Cabot Lodge was one. Jacob Riis was another. And of course he was entirely transparent with Edith and his children.

Like anyone who is constantly thrust into the public eye, he was able to maintain a wide circle of relationships through a generous application of the social graces. But he simultaneously guarded his private affairs, maintaining genuine intimacy only with those whom he could trust implicitly.

A Pro-Life Stalwart

Never will I sit motionless while directly or indirectly apology is made for the murder of the helpless.[139]

THEODORE ROOSEVELT WAS CONVINCED that the family was the fundamental cornerstone of society. Anything that eroded the family's strength or vitality, anything that sought to undermine its authority or integrity, and anything that subverted its holy purpose or virtue was a dastardly threat to everything that he held to be good and right and true.

In his 1905 State of the Union address he highlighted his grave concern for America's deteriorating moral climate in general and the family's diminished cultural relevance, saying:

> The transformation of the family is one of the greatest sociological phenomena of our time; it is a social question of the first importance, of far greater importance than any merely political or economic question can be.[140]

He went on to describe a rather simple agenda for protecting the family against the encroachment of those men and women he called "the foes of our own household."[141] He said:

There are those who believe that a new modernity demands a new morality. What they fail to consider is the harsh reality that there is no such thing as a new morality. There is only one morality. All else is immorality. There is only true Christian ethics over against which stands the whole of paganism. If we are to fulfill our great destiny as a people, then we must return to the old morality, the sole morality.[142]

His analysis was utterly scathing:

All these blatant sham reformers, in the name of a new morality, preach the old, old vice and self-indulgence which rotted out first the moral fiber and then even the external greatness of Greece and Rome.[143]

In a very real sense, Roosevelt was the original family values social conservative.

It is not surprising then, that when a new wave of abortion advocates made their way onto the American scene and into the public arena, Roosevelt was one of their chief opponents—in fact, apart from the hierarchy of the Catholic church, he was one of their only opponents.[144]

He railed against their "frightful and fundamental immorality," calling their cause a submission "to coldness, to selfishness, to love of ease, to shrinking from risk, and to an utter and pitiful failure in sense of perspective."[145] As he argued:

Artificially keeping families small inevitably involves prenatal infanticide and abortion—with all its pandering to self-indulgence, its shirking of duties, and its enervation of character.[146]

But he did not simply hurl invectives their way—he acted. He was instrumental in mobilizing Republicans, Democrats, and Progressives against the awful specter of commercial child-killing-building a solid coalition that was to resist the siren's call of abortion for another three-quarters of a century. As he said:

> The foes of our own household are our worst enemies; and we can oppose them, not only by exposing them and denouncing them, but by constructive work in planning and building reforms which shall take into account both the economic and the moral factors in human advance. We in America can attain our great destiny only by service; not by rhetoric, and above all not by insincere rhetoric, and that dreadful mental double-dealing and verbal juggling which makes promises and repudiates them, and says one thing at one time, and the directly opposite thing at another time. Our service must be the service of deeds.[147]

He went on to assert:

> The most dangerous form of sentimental debauch is to give expression to good wishes on behalf of virtue while you do nothing about it. Justice is not merely words. It is to be translated into living acts.[148]

The infamous Margaret Sanger, who founded the vast Planned Parenthood abortion network, rightly saw Roosevelt as "a holdover from the old Christian religion," and thus a serious obstacle to her revolutionary program that called for "no gods and no masters."[149] She railed against him as "a disgraceful blight upon any modern scientific nation's intent to advance."[150]

For a leader who had staked his reputation and risked his career for the sake of traditional family values, that was high praise indeed. For no commendation can be greater than the condemnation of one's fiercest sworn enemies.

Progressive

A great democracy must be progressive or it will soon cease to be a democracy.[151]

AT THE TURN OF the century, the urgent problems brought on by dramatic changes in the social and cultural landscape—rampant industrialization, mass urbanization, and sudden class dispossession—demanded immediate and innovative solutions. The progressive movement was a cultural and political phenomenon that arose to offer such solutions.

At first the movement was nonpartisan and nonideological. It was simply a coalition of reform-minded individuals who came from every walk of life and from every political persuasion imaginable. They were united only in their concern for such things as industrial safety, child labor, tenement sanitation, building standards, property rights, food purity guidelines, commercial integrity, tax restructuring, family dispossession, and market monopolization.

According to Roosevelt, the credo of this diverse movement was fairly straightforward and simple:

It is our business to show that nine-tenths of wisdom consists in being wise in time. Woe to our nation if we let matters drift, if in our industrial and political life we let an unchecked and utterly selfish individualistic materialism riot to its appointed end. That end would be widespread disaster, for it would mean that our people would be sundered by those dreadful lines of division which are drawn when the selfish greed of the haves is set over against the selfish greed of the have-nots. There is but one way to prevent such a division, and that is to forestall it by the kind of movement in which we are now engaged.[152]

The aim was not to reinvent politics—or even the existing political parties and structures—but to provide an impetus for cooperative and harmonious reform for the good of all:

Our movement is one of resolute insistence upon the rights and full acknowledgment of the duties of every man and every woman within this great land of ours. We war against the forces of evil, and the weapons we use are the weapons of right. We do not set greed against greed or hatred against hatred. Our creed is one that bids us to be just to all, to feel sympathy for all, and to strive for an understanding of the needs of all. Our purpose is to smite down wrong. But to those who have done the wrong we feel only the kindliest charity that is compatible with causing the wrong to cease. We preach hatred to no man, and the spirit in which we work is as far removed from vindictiveness as from weakness. We are resolute to do away with the evil, and we intend to proceed with such wise and cautious sanity as will cause the very minimum of disturbance that is compatible with achieving our purpose.[153]

Under his dynamic leadership at home—and with the English Distributist writer Hilaire Belloc leading the charge abroad—the movement produced a powerful groundswell of united support for

sweeping social, political, and economic reforms. Rights were secured for organized labor; political machines were called into account; civil rights were ensured; health and safety standards were
instituted; small commercial interests were protected; and massive
corporate trusts were reined in.

Despite remarkable successes in achieving its immediate aims
however, progressivism was short-lived—at least as a single united
movement. With success came the inevitable bickering and backbit-
ing. The movement quickly splintered into wildly divergent special
interest factions. In America, once Roosevelt left his "bully pulpit"
in the White House, Henry Cabot Lodge and Charles Lindbergh Sr.
valiantly tried to carry on progressivism's tradition—as informed by
Christian conviction, patriotism, and family values. In Europe, once
Belloc left his seat in the House of Commons, Cecil Chesterton and
Maurice Baring likewise attempted to uphold progressivism's Distributist legacy. In both cases, however, the bulk of the once mighty
movement began to dissipate.

The fact is, among the movement's disparate factions and interests, there were a large number of irreverent and impatient young
radicals who were guided by a very different ideological standard:
the revolutionary philosophies and ideals of the humanistic Enlightenment. They pushed the bulk of progressivism into the fringes
of Western politics and culture, establishing dozens of groups intent
on the utter decimation of Christendom's vision of life, liberty, and
the pursuit of happiness: the mugwumps, the anarchists, the
Knights of Labor, the Grangers, the single-taxers, the suffragettes,
the International Workers of the World, the populists, and the
communists. What had begun as a conservative social movement
for reform had spun out of control and become the motley aggrega-
tion of liberal activism.

As Roosevelt once quipped, "Every reform movement has a lunatic fringe."[154]

The lunatic fringe, more than any other factor, caused the sudden dissipation of progressive influence following the defeat of its ticket in 1912. Roosevelt himself remained committed to the conservative ideals of the early movement, but he was forced to admit to the single greatest error of his storied career: he believed that he could carry the weight of the movement on his own considerable shoulders.

His failure to do so forced him to recognize the fact that social movements need far more than a gifted or popular leader. They need a consensus wrought by a common world view and a common faith.

Prejudice

I should hang my head in shame if I were capable of discriminating against a man because he and I have different shades of skin. [155]

ROOSEVELT HAD AN ACUTE sense of justice, fairness, and propriety. Though he was often accused of being a jingo and an ethnic elitist, he actually despised all manner of discrimination. He found prejudice intolerable. And he simply could not fathom how anyone—much less a professing Christian—could condone rank racism.

At a time when public men—and especially politicians—were either reticent to discuss matters of race or altogether mum, he was startlingly forthright in his pronouncements:

> The wise and honorable and Christian thing to do is to treat each black man and each white man on his merits as a man, giving him no more and no less than he shows he is worthy to have. [156]

He was convinced of the equality of all men—though certainly not of all cultures—and only asked that individuals adhere to the principles and precepts of Christendom in order to partake equally of the benefits of society:

Above all we must stand shoulder to shoulder, not asking as to the ancestry or creed of our comrades, but only demanding that they be in very truth Americans, and that we all work together, heart, hand, and head, for the honor and the greatness of our common country.[157]

Once when he was the police commissioner of New York, this equanimity was put to the test. Rector Ahlwardt, a notorious German anti-Semite, came to the city for a series of meetings. Roosevelt was caught in quite a conundrum:

A great many of the Jews became alarmed and incensed about his speaking here, and called upon me to prevent it. Of course, I told them I could not—that the right of free speech must be maintained, and that unless he incited to riot, he would be allowed to speak against the Jews just as we should let Jews speak against Christians.[158]

At the same time, his sense of justice would not allow him to leave the situation at that, so he very creatively stamped the impress of his moral tenor on the difficult circumstance:

On thinking it over, it occurred to me that there was one way in which I could undo much of the mischief he was trying to do, and I directed that so far as possible the policemen detailed to protect him at his meetings should themselves be Jews. This done, and Herr Ahlwardt delivered his violent harangues against the men of Hebrew faith, owing his safety to the fact that he was scrupulously protected by men of the very race which he was denouncing.[159]

The great racial divide in America—then as now—was between black and white. But Roosevelt was among the first political figures to evidence an attitude of racial equality and a defense of civil rights:

It was my good fortune at Santiago to serve beside black troops. A man who is good enough to shed his blood for his country is good enough to be given a square deal afterward. More than that no man is entitled to, and less than that no man shall have.[160]

When he was president, he caused a furor when he invited his friend Booker T. Washington to dine with him in the White House. The renowned black educator was the founder of the Tuskegee Institute in Alabama and was one of the most eloquent public speakers in America. In addition, he was well acquainted with Southerners of both races and was a good judge of men. As a result, Roosevelt had relied upon him for some time for advice in selecting candidates, both black and white, to fill federal positions in the region. When it was reported that the president and his wife had entertained a black man in the White House—a historic first—a wave of protests were touched off in both the North and the South. The *Memphis Scimitar* termed the dinner "the most damnable outrage ever."[161] One senator even asserted that the nation's capital had become "so saturated with the odor of the n[—] that the rats have taken refuge in the stables."[162]

Rather naive on the whole issue, Roosevelt was quite surprised by the hostile reaction:

I had no thought whatever of anything save of having a chance of showing some little respect to a man whom I cordially esteem as a good citizen and a good American. The outburst of feeling is to me literally inexplicable. It does not anger me. As far as I am personally concerned I regard their attacks with the most contemptuous indifference, but I am very melancholy that such feeling should exist in such bitterly aggravated form.[163]

In the end, Roosevelt stuck by his guns, asserting with typical epigrammatic precision, "Better faithful than famous."[164]

Heroes

A nation needs heroes. It needs examples of valor so that it will know just how it ought to behave.[165]

ROOSEVELT ALWAYS HAD DIFFICULTY seeing himself as a hero. But that was merely because he was modest. He certainly did not abide by the peculiarly modern notion that men should cynically avoid heroes. He was particularly enamored with a large number of heroes from the past:

> From reading of the people I admired—ranging from the soldiers of Valley Forge and [Daniel] Morgan's riflemen to my Southern forefathers and kinfolk—I felt a great admiration for men who were fearless and who could hold their own in the world. And I had a great desire to be like them.[166]

Many of his heroes were rather typical. He held George Washington and Abraham Lincoln in great esteem, for instance. He was also terribly fond of Alexander Hamilton, Patrick Henry, Stonewall Jackson, Daniel Boone, Robert E. Lee, and George Rogers Clark.

In addition though, he greatly admired a number of rather less likely heroes. As an avid reader of Walter Scott's *Waverley* novels, he had developed a tremendous affection for William Wallace, Robert the Bruce, and Bonnie Prince Charlie. Scott's *Ivanhoe* was a personal favorite—and so he had long been intrigued with the Crusaders, particularly Richard the Lion-Hearted. He was also an unabashed admirer of England's most revered kings—including Arthur, Alfred the Great, and Henry V.

His research and writing had made him particularly fond of Gouverneur Morris, Thomas Hart Benton, and Oliver Cromwell—all of whom became subjects of his biographical labors. And of course he fairly idolized the men who won the West—such as James Robertson, John Sevier, and Meriwether Lewis.

When he and Henry Cabot Lodge wrote their *Hero Tales from American History*, they said their only desire was "to tell in simple fashion the story of some Americans who showed that they knew how to live and how to die; who proved their truth by their endeavor; and who joined to the stern and manly qualities which are essential to the well-being of a masterful people the virtues of gentleness, of patriotism, and of lofty adherence to an ideal."[167]

Indeed, they argued:

It is a good thing for all Americans, and it is an especially good thing for all young Americans, to remember the men who have given their lives in war and peace to the service of their fellow countrymen, and to keep in mind the feats of daring and personal prowess done in time past by some of the many champions of the nation in the various crises of her history.[168]

Lodge later recalled that Roosevelt was especially concerned to set out for ordinary Americans a model of patriotic decorum by portraying the lives, careers, and achievements of their greatest forebears:

He wanted all men to be able to readily ascertain the chief ingredients of greatness and valor. He wanted to illustrate how thrift, industry, obedience to law, fulfillment of duty, and intellectual cultivation are essential qualities in the makeup of any successful people. He wanted to provide others with heroes such as had heretofore faithfully guided him through the many shallows and shoals of his own life and career. He wanted all Americans to benefit as he had from the giants of valor.[169]

Of course Roosevelt's first and greatest hero was his own father. Throughout his life he confessed that his chief aim was to live up to the standard of honor, courage, and integrity that had been established for him. Because of his relationship with his father, Roosevelt had early come to understand that all leaders must first be led. Because of his relationship with his father, he had early come to understand that every hero must have his own heroes.

He lived his life as a sincere imitator of the best attributes of others—and so became a model for all those who have come after him.

Bullfeathers

Profanity is the parlance of the fool. Why curse
when there is such a magnificent language with which
to discourse?[170]

EVERYONE AGREED THAT Theodore Roosevelt lived one of the most colorful lives of his day. His activities were colorful. His ideals were colorful. His behavior was colorful. And he had a colorful vocabulary to match.

It seems that he took as much delight in the English language as he did everything else in life. And he made extraordinary use of it. His gift of phrase making was an integral aspect of his personality. Not surprisingly, much of his uniquely picturesque nomenclature—usually first uttered entirely off the cuff—has passed into common usage. Thus, we have "the larger good," "the square deal," "a straight shooter," "the hot potato," "the big stick" "mollycoddles and weaklings," "beaten to a frazzle," "the hat in the ring," "calling a spade a spade," "weasel words," "malefactors of great wealth," "how the West was won," "piffle pendants," and "strange bedfellows."[171]

He loved the art of neologism—making up new words to suit new occasions, often by combining old words or by transforming nouns into verbs. Thus we have "muckraking," "logothete," "tangibilitate,"

161

"pucksterism," "Baptistification," "driveler," "impuritanism," "bibble-babble," "intelligentry," "taftisn't," "acadenemic," and "wilsonizing."[172] His imagination was so rich that Gen. Leonard Wood often said that "he was so greedy for a proper expression of the truth that all the words in the dictionary were never enough for him."[173]

The one use of the language he could not tolerate, however, was profanity. According to his closest friend, Henry Cabot Lodge, "He never once indulged in the base language of the curse."[174] And according to his eldest son, "I never heard him utter a coarse or profane word—though he was often mad and unafraid to show it."[175]

Once after soon arriving in the Dakota Territory as a greenhorn cattleman, he confronted a cowboy with a bad habit of pouring forth a profusion of profanity. Bystanders began nervously moving away from the two—the man apparently had a reputation for a temper as foul as his mouth. He was wont to use his pistols at the slightest provocation. The rumor among the ranch hands was that he'd killed five men. Roosevelt was, as always, fearless. "A big man should never lower himself to small language," he told the renegade. He didn't flinch when the man fixed him with a ferociously threatening glare. But then, to everyone's amazement, the man dropped his eyes and admitted as much. "Perhaps you're right, Mr. Roosevelt," he sheepishly replied. "I'd best hold my tongue." Bill Sewall, a rough backwoods guide, later commented, "I've never seen anything like it. It was almost as if Roosevelt could just speak a word or two and wield a kind of moral command over everyone else around him."[176]

Thus, when others would resort to ribald expletives, Roosevelt would utter one of his famous substitutes. "Bully" was his favorite declaration. It expressed everything from joyous approval to enthusiastic surprise. "Bullfeathers" was another favorite assertion. Likewise, he often burst forth with "by Jove," "that's just dandy," "jolly good," "blast," "hup to," "shiver me timbers," "holy Toledo," and "goodness gracious."[177]

Roosevelt believed that language, like leadership, was an expression of character. To debase language is the inevitable result of an already debased character. To act shamefully is simply to reveal an already shameful estate. To dishonor and defile the conscience of another with rudeness or crudeness is merely the exposure of a dishonored and defiled character.

For him the responsibilities of leadership demanded positive clarity of expression—and excluded any possibility of crass abasement:

Before a man can discipline other men, he must demonstrate his ability to discipline himself. Before he may be allowed the command of commission, he must evidence command of character. Look then to the work of his hands. Hear the words of his mouth. By his fruit you shall know him.[178]

Faith

We stand at Armageddon and we battle for the Lord.[179]

WHATEVER THEODORE ROOSEVELT BELIEVED, he believed it strongly. His opinions were stated with the certainty of a creed. His policies were draped in the sanctity of revelation. That is simply because he had a very carefully worked-out world view, and his perspective of life was securely anchored to certain immutable articles of faith.

According to his own testimony, these articles of faith were defined by traditional Christian orthodoxy. "I am a Christian statesman," he often averred.[180] And thus he was "unable to accept the Pagan view of the world—or even that of Humanism."[181] To his mind the Christian world view was a comprehensive frame of reference touching the totality of life, not simply the hazy zone of personal piety. Christianity was for him not merely a plan of salvation, an ethical system, or an exercise in mysticism. It was truth. It was truth about all things for all men at all times.

Thus he urged the American people to be ever vigilant in the maintenance of their faith. Indeed, he was fearful of any sort of lapse of authentic Christian expression among the citizenry:

No abounding of material prosperity shall avail us if our spiritual senses atrophy. The foes of our own household will surely prevail against us unless there be in our people an inner life which finds its outer expression in a morality like unto that preached by the seers and prophets of God when the grandeur that was Greece and the glory that was Rome still lay in the future.[182]

Like so much else in his character and thought, his faith was inculcated early in his life by his beloved father:

Morning prayers were with my father. We used to stand at the foot of the stairs, and when father came down we called out, "I speak for you and the cubby-hole too!" There were three of us young children, and we used to sit with father on the sofa while he conducted morning prayers. The place between father and the arm of the sofa we called the "cubby-hole." The child who got that place we regarded as especially favored both in comfort and somehow in rank and title.[183]

He observed all the conventions of his Dutch Reformed background and taught them to his children. He attended church regularly. And from about 1876 on, he taught a Sunday school class whenever the opportunity arose. When questioned—as he often was by an inquisitive public—he quickly stated his doctrine was best summarized in the lyrics of his favorite hymn, "How Firm a Foundation":

How firm a foundation, you saints of the Lord,
Is laid for your faith in his excellent Word!
What more can He say than to you He has said,
To you who for refuge to Jesus have fled?

Fear not, I am with you, O be not dismayed,
For I am your God, and will still give you aid.

I'll strengthen you, help you, and cause you to stand,
Upheld by My righteous, omnipotent hand.

When through the deep waters I call you to go,
The rivers of water shall not overflow.
For I will be with you, your troubles to bless,
And sanctify to you your deepest distress.

When through fiery trials your pathway shall lie,
My grace, all sufficient, shall be your supply.
The flame shall not hurt you; I only design,
Your dross to consume and your gold to refine.

E'en down to old age all my people shall prove,
My sovereign, eternal, unchangeable love.
And when hoary hair shall their temples adorn,
Like lambs they shall still in my bosom be born.

The soul that on Jesus has leaned for repose,
I will not, I will not desert to his foes.
That soul, though all hell should endeavor to shake,
I'll never, no never, no never forsake.[184]

Believing that all leadership is in the end moral leadership, Roosevelt was convinced that a leader's faith must be firmly established. Quite obviously, his was.

The Bible

I try to avoid that species of intensely offensive spiritual pride which takes the form of sniggering conceit in being heterodox. [185]

THEODORE ROOSEVELT STOOD FOURSQUARE on the legacy of biblical orthodoxy. He often asserted that he was "proud of his Holland, Huguenot, and Covenanting ancestors, and proud that the blood of that stark Puritan divine Jonathan Edwards flows in the veins of my children." [186]

This strongly affirmed Reformed heritage centered on a determined reverence for the comprehensive authority of the Bible in its applicability to both the spiritual life and material life. It was a fully integrated tradition that recognized the Bible's relevance to sociology as well as salvation, to reform as well as redemption, and to culture as well as conversion.

Thus he made Bible reading and Bible study a vital part of his daily life, and he encouraged others to likewise partake of its great wisdom. "A thorough knowledge of the Bible," he argued, "is worth more than a college education." [187]

Again, the reason for this was not simply that the Bible outlined a good and acceptable system of personal morals and social etiquette. He believed that the Bible was far more than that—that it was, in fact, the very warp and woof of the fabric of Western civilization. It was, therefore, an essential element of the maintenance of order, civility, and prosperity. Indeed, without it, the great American experiment in liberty would be thrown into very real jeopardy:

> Every thinking man, when he thinks, realizes that the teachings of the Bible are so interwoven and entwined with our whole civic and social life that it would be literally impossible for us to figure ourselves what that life would be if these standards were removed. We would lose almost all the standards by which we now judge both public and private morals; all the standards which we, with more or less resolution, strive to raise ourselves.[188]

He quoted the Bible often—evincing his intimate familiarity with it. One biographical archivist examined his published works and found he so had integrated Scripture into his thought processes, that there were actually more than forty-two hundred biblical images, references, inferences, or complete quotations contained therein. And his unpublished letters, articles, and speeches contained hundreds—perhaps even thousands—more.[189]

In 1902, during the height of an extremely tense diplomatic showdown with Britain and Germany over their forcible recovery of debt service in Venezuela, several key military advisers were summoned to the White House. When they entered Roosevelt's office they found him furiously poring over a well-worn Bible and an exhaustive concordance. After a long and uncomfortable silence during which the president never acknowledged their presence, one of the generals cleared his throat and addressed the great man, "You asked for us, sir?" Without looking up from the volumes before him the president responded, "Well, don't just stand there men. I need help. I can't remember why I hold to the Monroe Doctrine. I know that it's got to be in here somewhere." Still not quite comprehending what he wanted them to do, the men moved toward his desk, whereupon the president handed each of them a Bible to peruse. "Get to work, men," he told them. "I can't act without warrant. I can't pronounce policy without precedence or precept."[190]

Roosevelt believed that there were absolutes. To his mind true leadership must always be accountable to that set of unchanging principles—ones not affected by the movement of the clock or the advance of the calendar. And he believed that those absolute principles could only reliably be found in the Book of Books—the Bible.

The Church

A churchless society is most assuredly a society on the downgrade.[191]

ROOSEVELT WAS AN ENTHUSIASTIC churchman. He grew up in the church, raised his children in the church, and remained in the church until his dying day. He did not "think much of a religion so internalized and subjective that it found no expression in outward corporate worship."[192] His reasoning was simple and straightforward: "Man was made for covenant."[193]

His personal experience with the church was a happy one—and he drew great strength from it. As he confessed to his friends, "After a week of wrestling with perplexing problems, it does so rest my soul to come into the house of the Lord and to sing—and to mean it— Holy, Holy, Holy, Lord God Almighty."[194]

In ordinary times, in times of crisis, and in times of ecstasy and joy, Roosevelt found himself most comfortable in the midst of the fellowship of faith. It was there that he was refreshed in his charge to defend the values, virtues, and vision that had made America the last great bastion of Christian civilization:

There are those who believe that a new modernity demands a new morality. What they fail to consider is the harsh reality that there is no such thing as a new morality. There is only one morality. All else is immorality. There is only true Christian ethics over against which stands the whole of paganism. If we are to fulfill our great destiny as a people, then we must return to the old morality, the sole morality. And if we are to do that, then the church must prepare us for such a task.[195]

But even apart from these essentially spiritual and covenantal concerns, Roosevelt believed that the institutional church played an essential function in American society and culture. His study of history had convinced him that without the active interplay of its salt and light, communities inevitably began to decay:

> In the pioneer days of the West we found it an unfailing rule that after a community had existed for a certain length of time either a church was built or else the community began to go down hill. In those old communities in the Eastern States which have gone backward, it is noticeable that the retrogression has been both marked by and accentuated by a rapid decline in church membership and work; the two facts being so interrelated that each stands to the other partly as a cause and partly as an effect.[196]

Though he was a bit of a freethinker when it came to theological issues—at times advocating rather marginal positions on key points of dogma—he was not favorably disposed toward liberal or neoorthodox theology. Chief among the reasons was that such theology seemed to undermine the stability of a congregation's ongoing mission in the community and the world. Thus he was an outspoken advocate for tradition—both in practice and belief. He even strove to honor the injunction to "keep the Sabbath." He always refrained from hunting, fishing, playing games, or transacting any sort of business on Sunday.

In addition, he was active as a witness to his faith, regularly inviting his friends to attend church with him. When John Willis—who had initiated him into the rough-and-tumble ways of frontier living—claimed to have made a man of him, Roosevelt replied, "Yes, John made a man out of me, but I made a Christian out of John. I actually had to drag him kicking and screaming into the church house the first few times."[197]

When his eldest child Alice became a teenager, she went through a difficult period of rebellion. In particular, she had decided that church was just "humbug." One Sunday morning at Sagamore Hill she simply refused to dress and prepare herself for the morning worship services. Roosevelt told her in no uncertain terms that he would not tolerate "infidels" in his home.[198]

He recognized that by the very nature of his task as a parent, he had to impose his will upon his children at times. That is actually the essence of leadership: to move people in a direction that they would not ordinarily go of their own accord—but in which they must go if they are to attain to their own peculiar calling.

Alice went to church that morning and every Sunday afterward.

TR and FDR

*Woe to the man or to the nation that stands as once
Laodicea stood; as the people of ancient Meroz stood,
when they dared not come to the help of the Lord against
the mighty.*[199]

THERE ARE TWO FIGURES that dominated the American scene in the twentieth century. The first was Theodore Roosevelt. The second, remarkably, was his young cousin, Franklin Roosevelt. Both men possessed great personal charisma, keen political instincts, penetrating social consciences, seemingly boundless energy, and brilliantly diverse intellects. Both of them left a lasting impress upon the world. But that is where the similarity between the two ends. In every other way, they could not have been more different.[200]

Franklin Roosevelt was the patriarch of the Hyde Park side of the family. A Harvard-educated lawyer, he began his political career as a Democratic Party reformer in the New York State Senate. His vigorous campaign on behalf of Woodrow Wilson—against his famous cousin—during the 1912 presidential election earned him an appointment as assistant secretary of the navy. In 1920 he was the vice presidential running mate on the losing Democratic ticket. Eight years later, after a crippling bout with polio, he was elected to the first of two terms as New York's governor. Finally, in 1932, he ran for the presidency against the Depression-plagued Herbert Hoover and won overwhelmingly. During his record four terms, he directed the ambitious transformation of American government, created the modern system of social welfare, guided the nation through World War II, and laid the foundations for the United Nations.

Theodore Roosevelt was a conservative social reformer who wanted to firmly and faithfully reestablish the "Old World Order."[201] Franklin Roosevelt, on the other hand, was a liberal social revolutionary who wanted to boldly and unashamedly usher in the "New World Order."[202]

Theodore Roosevelt's motto was "speak softly and carry a big stick."[203] Franklin Roosevelt's motto was "good neighbors live in solidarity."[204]

Theodore Roosevelt spoke forcefully but led the world into a remarkable epoch of peace—he even won the Nobel Peace Prize in 1905. Like his mentor, Woodrow Wilson, Franklin Roosevelt spoke of peace but led the world into the bloodiest confrontation in man's tortured history.

The difference between the two perspectives was fundamental and presuppositional. Whereas Franklin Roosevelt's liberal global vision was informed by an unhesitatingly humanistic world view, Theodore Roosevelt's conservative civic vision was informed by an uncompromising Christian world view. In fact, while Franklin Roosevelt rejected the faith of his fathers early in his life, Theodore Roosevelt held tenaciously to the spiritual legacy that had been passed on to him by his father and grandfather. He often reveled in his Dutch Reformed and Scottish Covenanter roots. And the family ties to "that stark Puritan divine Jonathan Edwards" was for him a point of special pride.[205]

The practical outworking of these two models for American life and culture was dramatic: Franklin Roosevelt's led to invasive bureaucracy at home and intrusive adventurism abroad, while Theodore Roosevelt's led to progressive grass-roots reform at home and sagacious cooperation abroad. Franklin Roosevelt's vision paved the way for modern liberalism, accommodationism, federal interventionism, and the New Left. Theodore Roosevelt's vision paved the way for modern conservatism, anti-communism, communitarian responsibility, and the New Right.

Both men understood the very critical notion that ideas have consequences. As a result, the twentieth century in America has largely been the tale of two households—of the Roosevelts of Sagamore Hill and of the Roosevelts of Hyde Park.

Sagamore Hill

At Sagamore Hill we love a great many things—birds and trees and books and all things beautiful, children and gardens and hard work and the joy of life.[206]

LIKE ULYSSES, THEODORE ROOSEVELT had seen all the wonder of the world. He traveled extensively throughout North America, Europe, Africa, the Middle East, and Central and South America. He enjoyed his stays amid the hustle and bustle of the world's greatest cities. And he relished his opportunities to tramp about in the world's most untamed wildernesses. But his lifelong conviction was that for all the majesty, splendor, mystery of those distant realms, there was no place like home.

Home for him was Sagamore Hill. It was the home he had designed and built overlooking Oyster Bay on Long Island. It was a spacious old-fashioned house surrounded by wide porches and punctuated with a bevy of large fireplaces. Its shingled exterior was notable for its profusion of gables and chimneys, while the interior boasted large rooms with high ceilings, dark Edwardian furnishings, and dozens of hunting trophies in every available nook and cranny.

In every way the house reflected the personality of the larger-than-life family that occupied it. Jacob Riis testified that it "fairly shouted the vim, vigor, and vitality of its proprietors."[207]

Through the years the house served as a mecca for the distinguished men of the age. It was the meeting place for those whose ideas, actions, and intentions animated the time with optimism and confidence. Scientists, naturalists, thinkers, writers, artists, statesmen, reformers, and businessmen gathered there to imbibe the atmosphere and to sit in the proximity of their greatest champion and mentor.

It was there at Sagamore Hill that the military strategy for the Spanish-American War was hammered out. It was there that the progressive movement was birthed. It was there that the determination to build the Panama Canal was confirmed. And it was there that the "carry a big stick" policy was first conceived.

But as much as the home served as the hub of national and international activity, it was also Roosevelt's refuge from the cares of the world. Until he became president he refused to have a phone installed in the place. The house was his getaway, his refuge, and his solace.

Originally sitting on more than a hundred acres, the property was a haven of rest for him. He could think there. He could rest there. He could enjoy his children—and later his grandchildren—there. And he could enjoy his beloved outdoors there. He considered it "the one place on earth where the affairs of this poor fallen world very nearly seem to be set aright."[208]

Often Roosevelt would spend hours sitting on the front porch, simply rocking. Of course, for him, simply rocking took on a whole new definition: he rocked his chair so vigorously that it would traverse the entire length of the porch. Edith often scolded him for his hyperactivity. He just replied, "You relax your way, I'll relax mine."[209]

At the end of his life, he took special comfort in his home. Tired from his many battles, enfeebled by his injuries and illnesses, and

frustrated by the foolhardiness of the Wilson administration's han-
dling of vital issues of national interest, Roosevelt often retreated to
his library and porches to think, reflect, convalesce, and rest.

The night he died, his final words to Edith were, "I wonder if you
will ever know how I love Sagamore Hill."[210]

He knew better than most that leaders must have a sanctuary in
which to retreat. There is, indeed, no place like home.

American Spirit

*In the fight for Americanism there must be no
sagging back.*[211]

THEODORE ROOSEVELT'S SEEMINGLY COMPULSIVE busyness was not mere hyperactivity. Nor was it the fruit of some primordial workaholism. Instead, labor was the natural product of what he called "the strenuous life."[212] For him it was both a philosophy of life and a sense of mission:

> I always believe in going hard at everything. My experience is that it pays never to let up or grow slack and fall behind.[213]

Once Jacob Riis visited Roosevelt at the governor's residence in Albany. He was taken to the basement where the great man was getting a shave and a haircut. In order to keep busy, he was straddling a lap desk across his knees so that he could catch up on his correspondence. Simultaneously, he had three secretaries arrayed around him to whom he was dictating in alternating paragraphs. To one he was composing the final chapters of his biography of Oliver Cromwell, to another he was outlining portions of his upcoming legislative agenda, and to the third he was drafting a speech he would give later in the afternoon. All while writing on his lap and receiving a shave and a haircut! Riis could hardly believe his eyes. Riis asked him how he could possibly do so much at once. Roosevelt shrugged and responded that he was simply trying "to make the most of the time."[214]

For him the injunction to "make the most of every opportunity" was a nonnegotiable imperative predicated not on his abilities and gifts but on his calling and faithfulness.[215] His life was lived according to the dictates, "Get action! Don't flinch! Don't foul! Hit the line hard!"[216] In fact, he believed that all his accomplishments were attributable to his early apprehension of this principle rather than any propensity to greatness that he may have inherited or inculcated.

This was, in fact, his understanding of the special American spirit. It was a kind of national exceptionalism rooted in vision, effort, and valor:

> America has not attained to greatness because of what we are or what we have. We have become the exemplars of all the world because of what we have done with what we are and what we have.[217]

He believed that kind of achievement brought with it a responsibility—one that could not be shirked but at great hazard to all:

> Our place must be great among the nations. We may either fail greatly or succeed greatly; but we cannot avoid the endeavor from which either great failure or great success must come. Even if we would we cannot play a small part. If we should try, all that would follow would be that we should play a large part ignobly.[218]

Some called his attitude jingoism, others patriotism, and still others simply enthusiasm. But for Roosevelt his conception of

American nationalism was the capstone of his whole philosophy of life:

> America was not born of a single people or a single tradition or a single movement. Rather, our nation was born of a single idea—one that transcends the mere material attachments of other ethnicities. Our nation was born of the peculiar notion that all men were born to be free. Thus, America is the best expression of the highest aspiration of mankind. Best we safeguard such a sacred trust for all other nations with all the fervor and ardor we can muster. Therein lies the American Spirit.[219]

All his ebullience for American ingenuity, all his enthusiasm for American achievement, and all his exuberance for American valor was merely an expression of this idea: that with great privileges come great responsibilities, that blessings bring with them duties, and that the joy of liberty is the most sober obligation ever entrusted to men or nations.

The Legacy of
Theodore Roosevelt

> The world is at this moment passing through one of those
> terrible periods of convulsion when the souls of men and
> of nations are tried as by fire. . . . In such a crisis the
> moral weakling is the enemy of the right, the enemy of
> life, liberty, and the pursuit of happiness.[1]

The Micah Mandate

> The most dangerous form of sentimental debauch is to
> give expression to good wishes on behalf of virtue while
> you do nothing about it. Justice is not merely words. It is
> to be translated into acts.[2]

IN 1917, WHEN AMERICAN troops were preparing to sail across the
seas in order to take to the battlefields of France and Belgium in the
First World War, the New York Bible Society asked Roosevelt to in-
scribe a message in the pocket New Testaments that each of the soldiers would be given. The great man happily complied. And he
began by quoting a striking biblical call for a life of balance—what
he called the "Micah Mandate."[3]

> He has shown you, O man, what is good and what the Lord requires of
> you: but to do justice, and to love mercy, and to walk humbly with your
> God. (Micah 6:8)

Saying "the whole teaching of the New Testament [is] foreshad-
owed in Micah's verse," Roosevelt exhorted the men to lead the
world in "both word and deed" through unimpeachable moral up-
rightness.[4] In his brief message to the soldiers, he explained:

Do justice; and therefore fight valiantly against those that stand for the reign of Moloch and Beelzebub on this earth. Love mercy; treat your enemies well; succor the afflicted; treat every woman as if she were your sister; care for the little children; and be tender with the old and helpless. Walk humbly; you will do so if you study the life and teachings of the Savior, walking in His steps.[5]

He concluded, saying:

Remember: the most perfect machinery of government will not keep us as a nation from destruction if there is not within us a soul. No abounding of material prosperity shall avail us if our spiritual senses atrophy. The foes of our own household will surely prevail against us unless there be in our people an inner life which finds its outward expression in a morality like unto that preached by the seers and prophets of God when the grandeur that was Greece and the glory that was Rome still lay in the future.[6]

Roosevelt believed that the ultimate security of men and nations depended on a faithful adherence to the venerable Old Testament prophet's threefold demonstration of moral and practical balance: a strident commitment to justice, a tangible concern for mercy, and a reverent humility before the Almighty. He was certain that even with the deployment of superior forces in superior numbers with superior armaments, the American armies would ultimately be defeated during the war—if they took to the field bereft of this kind of personal integrity. And he was convinced that if individuals and families took only their limited material resources into the conflagration of our daily warfare, they too would be defeated and destroyed.

In his own life, these beacon lights of justice, mercy, and humility continually guided his steps—and they provide for us a key to understanding his great effectiveness as a leader.

Justice

FOR ROOSEVELT THE IDEA of justice was inextricably linked with the principle of righteousness. They were inseparable concepts as far as he was concerned. In both his public pronouncements and his private predilections, he made it plain that any attempt to secure justice, whether at home, in the community, or among the nations—any attempt apart from the clearly revealed ethical parameters of goodness, truth, purity, and faithfulness—would surely prove to be utter folly. On the other hand, he believed just as emphatically that any people that diligently sought to do right—to do righteousness—would inevitably pursue justice as well.

According to his very tightly conceived world view, the two simply went together. One could not be had without the other.

Again and again he sounded the refrain:

A true patriot must necessarily be a zealot and fighter for the truth. He must hold to the mean and enforce the dictates of righteousness with justice.[7]

187

Righteousness and justice flow on like a river—this then is the high call of freedom.[8]

The golden middle course of liberty is held by the crusader for truth with the sword of righteousness in one hand and the trowel of justice in the other.[9]

Roosevelt was thoroughly convinced that there could be no standard for the outward life if there were no standard for the inward life. But, simultaneously, there could be no inward standard if there were no outward standard. For him, justice and righteousness were completely inseparable.

Gouverneur Morris was one of Roosevelt's heroes; the biography he wrote of the great merchant, lawyer, and planter from Pennsylvania was one of his earliest literary and historical triumphs. Morris—who was actually responsible for the draft version of the Constitution—believed, with Alexander Hamilton, Patrick Henry, George Washington, and many of the other framers, that in order for the American experiment in liberty to succeed, justice and righteousness had to be "welded together as one in the hearts and minds of the citizenry."[10] Thus he said:

Liberty and justice simply cannot be had apart from the gracious influences of a righteous people. A righteous people simply cannot exist apart from the aspiration to liberty and justice. The Christian religion and its incumbent morality is tied to the cause of freedom with a Gordian knot; loose one from the other and both are sent asunder.[11]

The influence of Morris on Roosevelt was, quite understandably, great. So, according to his conception, good citizenship and personal virtue were essential aspects of the same bolt of fabric. He could tolerate no distinction between the inward and outward, the heart and the hand, the soul and the body—thus his affinity for the "Micah Mandate."

> He has shown you, O man, what is good and what the Lord requires of you: but to do justice, and to love mercy, and to walk humbly with your God. (Micah 6:8)

Mercy

IN THE SAME WAY that Roosevelt associated justice with the practice of righteousness, he linked mercy with the exercise of authority. They too were inseparable concepts in his carefully worked out scheme. He did not believe that authority could be had apart from mercy—and vice versa.

He was unflinching in his declaration: if any individuals were ever to influence their families or their culture to stand for goodness, faithfulness, and kindness, then they would have to graciously serve the hurts, wants, and needs all around them:

> The greatest men are those who would willingly serve in the shadows. The least and the last are the first and the foremost.[12]

> We must strive, each of us, so as to conduct our own lives as to be, to a certain extent at least, our brother's keeper.[13]

A life of authentic concern for the less privileged is the badge of authority in a culture. Acts of mercy are the only credentials for true greatness.[14]

This is one of the most basic principles of the leadership: the ability to lead a society is earned, not inherited. And it is earned through faithful, compassionate, and merciful service. Unfortunately, this principle has not been widely understood by most modern men and women—even by those of us who have been thrust into roles of grave responsibility.

In fact, the whole concept of servanthood—the high calling to exercise mercy—is a much neglected, largely forgotten vocation today. As a result, many of the gains and many of the distinctives of our culture have been needlessly eroded.

This is, after all, one of the greatest legacies the scions of Western civilization have passed on to us. It was the spirit of merciful service in the West that launched the first hospitals, orphanages, almshouses, soup kitchens, charitable societies, relief agencies, rescue missions, hostels, and shelters. And, as a result, that commitment to cooperation, accountability, and responsibility led Western civilization to new heights of freedom and prosperity for nearly two millennia.

Call it what you will—silk-stocking idealism, high-handed philanthropy, noblesse oblige, covenantal chivalry, or the square deal—Roosevelt was firmly convinced that mercy was an indispensable public and private virtue.

He has shown you, O man, what is good and what the Lord requires of you: but to do justice, and to love mercy, and to walk humbly with your God. (Micah 6:8)

Humility

THE TRADITIONAL CHRISTIAN APPROACH to any issue, or any problem, or any situation, or any circumstance—in fact, the traditional Christian approach to the whole of life—has always been theocentric. In other words, it begins and ends with and is ultimately centered in the Lord God Himself. He is, after all, the Alpha and the Omega of all things in reality. Thus for the orthodox to attempt any approach to reality without this in view is to invite frustration and failure. God is sovereign. This is the fundamental truth that underlies the whole of the Christian world view—from epistemology to soteriology. It comes as no surprise then that Roosevelt believed that a good man or woman's life should be entirely suffused with a holy fear and reverence of Him—to the point that everything else is thereby affected:

> If fear of the Almighty is the beginning of wisdom, then surely fear of the Almighty is the starting place of any fruitful endeavor.[15]

192

It is a humbling matter to consider the wide gulf, the gaping chasm that exists in this poor sin-besotted world between creature and Creator.[16]

Tremble in His midst so as to never falter in the midst of the grave responsibilities of life. Humility properly placed is the only sure foundation of leadership.[17]

Humility is not exactly a popular concept these days. Fernanda Eberstadt, in her brilliant coming-of-age novel *Isaac and His Devils* captured the prevailing sentiment of our time: "Humility has a dank and shameful smell to the worldly, the scent of failure, lowliness, and obscurity."[18]

But of course, such has not always been the case. In times past, humility was considered to be a virtue of supreme value. Applying this most fundamental truth to the arena of national and cultural integrity, George Washington asserted: "It is the first duty of all nations to acknowledge the providence of Almighty God, to obey His will, to be grateful for His benefits, and to humbly implore His protection and favor in holy fear."[19]

Roosevelt believed that, likewise, it was the first duty of all men and women.

He has shown you, O man, what is good and what the Lord requires of you: but to do justice, and to love mercy, and to walk humbly with your God. (Micah 6:8)

Our Need

At a memorial meeting in Philadelphia following the death of Theodore Roosevelt, Senator George Wharton Pepper summarized the import of the great man's legacy—his unflinching legacy of justice, mercy, and humility—to future generations:

> We as a people have sore need of Theodore Roosevelt. But not only collectively do we need him. We need him as individuals. When we look into our hearts we find that we shall have sustained a personal loss if we allow the Colonel to leave us. You and I need him as a factor in our daily lives. We have more energy when the Colonel is about. We are less content to submit to injustice, less appalled by obstacles in the path of progress. With the Colonel near we are far braver men and finer women. Where the Colonel leads we are sure of the direction in which we are moving. When he gives commands we are not in doubt about our objective. Happily, it will not be difficult to keep him with us. Theodore Roosevelt alive is easy to conceive of; Theodore Roo-

sevelt dead is altogether unthinkable. Such a man strengthens our belief in immortality. He has but gone to that front from which nobody
would dare to hold him back.[20]

He continued his eloquent eulogy, saying:

The immortality of personal influence is God's greatest gift to man.
When conscience cowers, when advice proves powerless, when reason
plays me false, his influence makes a man of me. I cannot cheat while
he is in the game. I cannot drift when he is headed upstream. I cannot
talk nonsense when he is there to hear. Dead? No. Today we are rejoic-
ing because Theodore Roosevelt is more alive than ever. There is not a
tinge of sadness in our celebration. The immortality of his influence
makes us glad with an exceeding great joy.[21]

Finally, he concluded by quoting the great man himself:

Just beyond man's narrow daily vision stand the immortals. And Jeho-
vah opened the eyes of the young man, and he saw; and behold, the
mountain was full of horses and chariots of fire about Elisha. At the
front of this nation's way ride the strong guards of our own past, their
authority immortalized by death. In the hour of decision we see them;
their grave eyes watch us, the keepers of our standards, the builders of
our freedom. They came from God to do His bidding—and returned.
To each of them the past has given his own labor. The future we cannot see; nor what the next imperious task; nor who its strong execu-
tant. But for this generation the task is clear: you who gird yourselves
for this great fight in the never-ending warfare for the good of
mankind, we stand at Armageddon and we battle for the Lord.[22]

The Lessons of Leadership

The hardest lessons to learn are those that are the most obvious.[23]

- The first prerequisite of true leadership is a happy home. The private life is the proving ground for the public life.

- Leadership must be modeled on some tangible, practical, and realizable ideal. Leaders have mentors. They are disciples. They comprehend the notion of legacy.

- Leaders are those who make the most of every moment, every opportunity, and every available resource.

- Leadership is the art of pursuing the ideal in the midst of a world that is something less than ideal.

- If you want to lead, you must read.

- A leader cannot lead a nation if he cannot vividly portray the path that he wishes to take.

- True leadership is a life committed to good deeds.

- A leader's goal, first and foremost, is to reach the goal.

- A leader is an idealist who is simultaneously blessed with a strong dose of reality.

- The role of the leader is to serve as a moral compass—pointing others toward justice and righteousness.

- A leader knows that what is really important in life rarely puts on airs of importance.

- There is little extraordinary about the achievements of a genius, a prodigy, or a savant. Inevitably, great leaders are those who overcome tremendous obstacles and still succeed.

- The essence of leadership is the ability to maintain great strength without any impulsive compulsion to use it. That strength is to be held in reserve, until and unless it becomes necessary to use it for the cause of right.

- A wise leader always uses whatever resources are placed at his disposal—but he never confuses the means with the ends.

- A leader will always attempt to unite others' disparate and distinctive legacies—and in so doing, help begin the vital process of healing.

- A leader has the ability to take any circumstance and see it through the lens of happy providence. He is living proof of the fact that laughter is indeed the best medicine.

- The efficacy of leadership depends, to a large degree, on the leader's incognizance of the negative consequences of doing right.

- A leader understands that failure is the backdoor to success.

- A leader is able to maintain a wide circle of relationships through a generous application of the social graces, but simultaneously guards his private affairs—maintaining genuine intimacy only with those whom he can trust implicitly.

- No commendation is greater than the condemnation of one's fiercest sworn enemies.

- Social movements need far more than a gifted or popular leader. They need a consensus wrought by a common world view and a common faith.

- A leader will always prefer to be faithful than famous.

- A leader invariably lives his life as a sincere imitator of the best attributes of others. Heroes always have heroes.

- The responsibilities of leadership demand positive clarity of expression—and exclude any possibility of crass abasement.

- Because all leadership is in the end moral leadership, a leader's faith must be firmly established.

- True leadership must always be accountable to that set of unchanging principles—ones that are not affected by the movement of the clock or the advance of the calendar.

- The essence of leadership is to move others in a direction they would not ordinarily go of their own accord—but which they must go if they are to attain to their own peculiar calling.

- Great leaders understand the very critical notion that ideas have consequences.

- Leaders must have a sanctuary in which to retreat. There is indeed no place like home.

- With great privileges come great responsibilities. Blessings bring with them duties. And the joy of liberty is the most sober obligation ever entrusted to men or nations.

Books for Holidays in the Open*

Here is a little taste of TR's writing. I've always loved the way this little essay displays his wide-ranging character, interests, and personality.

I AM sometimes asked what books I advise men or women to take on holidays in the open. With the reservation of long trips, where bulk is of prime consequence, I can only answer: The same books one would read at home. Such an answer generally invites the further question as to what books I read when at home. To this question I am afraid my answer cannot be so instructive as it ought to be, for I have never followed any plan in reading which would apply to all persons under all circumstances; and indeed it seems to me that no plan can be laid down that will be generally applicable. If a man is not fond of books, to him reading of any kind will be drudgery. I most sincerely commiserate such a person, but I do not know how to help him. If a man or a woman is fond of books he or she will naturally seek the books that the mind and soul demand. Suggestions of a possibly helpful character can be made by outsiders, but only suggestions; and they will probably be helpful about in proportion to the outsider's knowledge of the mind and soul of the person to be helped.

Of course, if any one finds that he never reads serious literature, if all his reading is frothy and trashy, he would do well to try to train himself to like books that the general agreement of cultivated and sound-thinking persons has placed among the classics. It is as discreditable to the mind to

---

*First published in *Ladies Home Journal*, April 1915.

be unfit for sustained mental effort as it is to the body of a young man to be unfit for sustained physical effort. Let man or woman, young man or girl, read some good author, say [Edward] Gibbon or [Thomas] Macaulay, until sustained mental effort brings power to enjoy the books worth enjoying. When this has been achieved the man can soon trust himself to pick out for himself the particular good books which appeal to him.

The equation of personal taste is as powerful in reading as in eating; and within certain broad limits the matter is merely one of individual preference, having nothing to do with the quality either of the book or of the reader's mind. I like apples, pears, oranges, pineapples, and peaches. I dislike bananas, alligator-pears, and prunes. The first fact is certainly not to my credit, although it is to my advantage; and the second at least does not show moral turpitude. At times in the tropics I have been exceedingly sorry I could not learn to like bananas, and on round-ups, in the cow country in the old days, it was even more unfortunate not to like prunes; but I simply could not make myself like either, and that was all there was to it.

In the same way I read over and over again "Guy Mannering," "The Antiquary," "Pendennis," "Vanity Fair," "Our Mutual Friend," and the "Pickwick Papers"; whereas I make heavy weather of most parts of the "Fortunes of Nigel," "Esmond," and the "Old Curiosity Shop"—to mention only books I have tried to read during the last month. I have no question that the latter three books are as good as the first six; doubtless for some people they are better; but I do not like them, any more than I like prunes or bananas.

In the same way I read and reread "Macbeth" and "Othello"; but not "King Lear" nor "Hamlet." I know perfectly well that the latter are as wonderful as the former—I wouldn't venture to admit my shortcomings regarding them if I couldn't proudly express my appreciation of the other two! But at my age I might as well own up, at least to myself, to my limitations, and read the books I thoroughly enjoy.

But this does not mean permitting oneself to like what is vicious or even simply worthless. If any man finds that he cares to read "Bel Ami," he will do well to keep a watch on the reflex centres of his moral nature, and to brace himself with a course of Eugene Brieux or Henry Bordeaux. If he does not care for "Anna Karenina," "War and Peace," "Sebastopol," and

"The Cossacks" he misses much; but if he cares for the "Kreutzer Sonata" he had better make up his mind that for pathological reasons he will be wise thereafter to avoid [Leo] Tolstoy entirely. Tolstoy is an interesting and stimulating writer, but an exceedingly unsafe moral adviser.

It is clear that the reading of vicious books for pleasure should be eliminated. It is no less clear that trivial and vulgar books do more damage than can possibly be offset by any entertainment they yield. There remain enormous masses of books, of which no one man can read more than a limited number, and among which each reader should choose those which meet his own particular needs. There is no such thing as a list of "the hundred best books," or the "best five-foot library."

Dozens of series of excellent books, one hundred to each series, can be named, all of reasonably equal merit and each better for many readers than any of the others; and probably not more than half a dozen books would appear in all these lists. As for a "five-foot library," scores can readily be devised, each of which at some given time, for some given man, under certain conditions, will be best. But to attempt to create such a library that shall be of universal value is foreordained to futility.

Within broad limits, therefore, the reader's personal and individual taste must be the guiding factor. I like hunting books and books of exploration and adventure. I do not ask any one else to like them. I distinctly do not hold my own preferences as anything whatever but individual preferences; and this chapter is to be accepted as confessional rather than didactic. With this understanding I admit a liking for novels where something happens; and even among these novels I can neither explain nor justify why I like some and do not like others; why, among the novels of [Henryk] Sienkiewicz, I cannot stand "Quo Vadis," and never tire of "With Fire and Sword," "Pan Michael," the "Deluge" and the "Knights of the Cross."

Of course, I know that the best critics scorn the demand among novel readers for "the happy ending." Now, in really great books—in an epic like [John] Milton's, in dramas like those of Aeschylus and Sophocles—I am entirely willing to accept and even demand tragedy, and also in some poetry that cannot be called great, but not in good, readable novels, of sufficient length to enable me to get interested in the hero and heroine!

There is enough of horror and grimness and sordid squalor in real life with which an active man has to grapple; and when I turn to the world of literature—of books considered as books, and not as instruments of my profession—I do not care to study suffering unless for some sufficient purpose. It is only a very exceptional novel which I will read if He does not marry Her; and even in exceptional novels I much prefer this consummation. I am not defending my attitude. I am merely stating it.

Therefore it would be quite useless for me to try to explain why I read certain books. As to how and when, my answers must be only less vague. I almost always read a good deal in the evening; and if the rest of the evening is occupied I can at least get half an hour before going to bed. But all kinds of odd moments turn up during even a busy day, in which it is possible to enjoy a book; and then there are rainy afternoons in the country in autumn, and stormy days in winter, when one's work outdoors is finished and after wet clothes have been changed for dry, the rocking-chair in front of the open wood-fire simply demands an accompanying book.

Railway and steamboat journeys were, of course, predestined through the ages as aids to the enjoyment of reading. I have always taken books with me when on hunting and exploring trips. In such cases the literature should be reasonably heavy, in order that it may last. You can under these conditions read Herbert Spencer, for example, or the writings of [A. R. J.] Turgot, or a German study of the Mongols, or even a German edition of Aristophanes, with erudite explanations of the jokes, as you never would if surrounded by less formidable authors in your own library; and when you do reach the journey's end you grasp with eager appetite at old magazines, or at the lightest of literature.

Then, if one is worried by all kinds of men and events—during critical periods in administrative office, or at national conventions, or during congressional investigations, or in hard-fought political campaigns—it is the greatest relief and unalloyed delight to take up some really good, some really enthralling book—Tacitus, Thucydides, Herodotus, Polybius, or [Johann Wolfgang von] Goethe, [John] Keats, [Thomas] Gray, or [James Russell] Lowell—and lose all memory of everything grimy, and of the baseness that must be parried or conquered.

Like every one else, I am apt to read in streaks. If I get interested in any subject I read different books connected with it, and probably also read books on subjects suggested by it. Having read [Thomas] Carlyle's "Frederick the Great"—with its splendid description of the battles, and of the unyielding courage and thrifty resourcefulness of the iron-tempered King; and with its screaming deification of able brutality in the name of morality, and its practice of the suppression and falsification of the truth under the pretense of preaching veracity—I turned to Macaulay's essay on this subject, and found that the historian whom it has been the fashion of the intellectuals to patronize or deride showed a much sounder philosophy and an infinitely greater appreciation of and devotion to truth than was shown by the loquacious apostle of the doctrine of reticence.

Then I took up [Richard] Waddington's "Guerre de Sept Ans"; then I read all I could about Gustavus Adolphus; and, gradually dropping everything but the military side, I got hold of quaint little old histories of Eugene of Savoy and [Henri] Turenne. In similar fashion my study of and delight in [Alfred Thayer] Mahan sent me further afield, to read queer old volumes about [Michel] De Ruyter and the daring warrior-merchants of the Hansa, and to study, as well as I could, the feats of [Pierre Andre de] Suffren and [Wilhelm von] Tegethoff. I did not need to study [David Glasgow] Farragut.

[J. P.] Mahaffy's books started me to reread—in translation, alas!—the post-Athenian Greek authors. After [Guglielmo] Ferrero I did the same thing as regards the Latin authors, and then industriously read all kinds of modern writers on the same period, finishing with [Charles William Chadwick] Oman's capital essay on "Seven Roman Statesmen." Gilbert Murray brought me back from Greek history to Greek literature, and thence by a natural suggestion to parts of the Old Testament, to the Nibelungenlied, to the Roland lay and the chansons de gestes, to Beowulf, and finally to the great Japanese hero-tale, the story of the Forty-Nine Ronins.

I read [John] Burroughs too often to have him suggest anything save himself; but I am exceedingly glad that Charles Sheldon has arisen to show what a hunter-naturalist, who adds the ability of the writer to the ability of the trained observer and outdoor adventurer, can do for our last great wilderness, Alaska. From Sheldon I turned to Stewart Edward White, and then began to wander afar, with Herbert Ward's "Voice from the Congo," and Mary Kingsley's writings, and [W. H.] Hudson's "El Ombu," and Cunningham Grahame's sketches of South America. A re-reading of The Federalist led me to [Edmund] Burke, to [George O.] Trevelyan's history of [Charles James] Fox and of our own Revolution, to [William E. H.] Lecky; and finally by way of [Thomas R.] Malthus and Adam Smith and Lord Acton and [Walter] Bagehot to my own contemporaries, to Ross and George Alger.

Even in pure literature, having nothing to do with history, philosophy, sociology, or economy, one book will often suggest another, so that one finds one has unconsciously followed a regular course of reading. Once I travelled steadily from [Michel Eyquem] Montaigne through [Joseph] Addison, [Jonathan] Swift, [Richard] Steele, [Charles] Lamb, [Washington] Irving, and [Robert] Lowell to Crothers and Kenneth Grahame—and if it be objected that some of these could not have suggested the others I can only answer that they did suggest them.

I suppose that every one passes through periods during which he reads no poetry; and some people, of whom I am one, also pass through periods during which they voraciously devour poets of widely different kinds. Now it will be Horace and [Alexander] Pope; now [Friedrich von] Schiller, [Walter] Scott, [Henry Wadsworth] Longfellow, [Karl Theodor] Körner; now Bret Harte or [Rudyard] Kipling; now {Percy Bysshe] Shelley or [Robert] Herrick or [Alfred] Tennyson; now [Edgar Allan] Poe and [Samuel Taylor] Coleridge; and again [Ralph Waldo] Emerson or [Robert] Browning or [Walt] Whitman. Sometimes one wishes to read for the sake of contrast. To me Owen Wister is the writer I wish when I am hungry with the memories of lonely mountains, of vast sunny plains with seas of wind-rippled grass, of springing wild creatures, and lithe, sun-tanned men who ride with utter ease on ungroomed, half-broken horses. But when I lived much in cow camps I often carried a volume of [Algernon Charles] Swinburne, as a kind of antiseptic to alkali dust, tepid, muddy water, frying-pan bread, sow-belly bacon, and the too-infrequent washing of sweat-drenched clothing.

Fathers and mothers who are wise can train their children first to practice, and soon to like, the sustained mental application necessary to enjoy good books. They will do well also to give each boy or girl the mastery of at least some one foreign language, so that at least one other great literature, in addition to our own noble English literature, shall be open to him or her. Modern languages are taught so easily and readily that whoever really desires to learn one of them can soon achieve sufficient command of it to read ordinary books with reasonable ease; and then it is a mere matter of practice for any one to become able thoroughly to enjoy the beauty and wisdom which knowledge of the new tongue brings.

Now and then one's soul thirsts for laughter. I cannot imagine any one's taking a course in humorous writers, but just as little can I sympathize with the man who does not enjoy them at times—from Sydney Smith to John Phoenix and Artemus Ward, and from these to Stephen Leacock. Mark Twain at his best stands a little apart, almost as much so as Joel Chandler Harris. Oliver Wendell Holmes, of course, is the laughing philosopher, the humorist at his very highest, even if we use the word "humor" only in its most modern and narrow sense.

A man with a real fondness for books of various kinds will find that his varying moods determine which of these books he at the moment needs. On the afternoon when [Robert Louis] Stevenson represents the luxury of enjoyment it may safely be assumed that [Edward] Gibbon will not. The mood that is met by [William F. P.] Napier's "Peninsular War," or [Baron de] Marbot's memoirs, will certainly not be met by [Nathaniel] Hawthorne or Jane Austen. [Francis] Parkman's "Montcalm and Wolfe," [John L.] Motley's histories of the Dutch Republic, will hardly fill the soul on a day when one turns naturally to the "Heimskringla"; and there is a sense of disconnection if after the "Heimskringla" one takes up the "Oxford Book of French Verse."

Another matter which within certain rather wide limits each reader must settle for himself is the dividing line between (1) not knowing anything about current books, and (2) swamping one's soul in the sea of vapidity which overwhelms him who reads only "the last new books." To me the heading employed by some reviewers when they speak of "books of the week" comprehensively damns both the books themselves and the reviewer who is willing to notice them. I would much rather see the heading "books of the year before last." A book of the year before last which is still worth noticing would probably be worth reading; but one only entitled to be called a book of the week had better be tossed into the wastebasket at once. Still, there are plenty of new books which are not of permanent value but which nevertheless are worth more or less careful reading; partly because it is well to know something of what especially interests the mass of our fellows, and partly because these books, although of ephemeral worth, may really set forth something genuine in a fashion which for the moment stirs the hearts of all of us.

Books of more permanent value may, because of the very fact that they possess literary interest, also yield consolation of a nonliterary kind. If any executive grows exasperated over the shortcomings of the legislative body with which he deals, let him study Macaulay's account of the way William was treated by his parliaments as soon as the latter found that, thanks to his efforts, they were no longer in immediate danger from foreign foes; it is illuminating. If any man feels too gloomy about the degeneracy of our people from the standards of their forefathers, let him read "Martin Chuzzlewit"; it will be consoling.

If the attitude of this nation toward foreign affairs and military preparedness at the present day seems disheartening, a study of the first fifteen years of the nineteenth century will at any rate give us whatever comfort we can extract from the fact that our great-grandfathers were no less foolish than we are.

Nor need any one confine himself solely to the affairs of the United States. If he becomes tempted to idealize the past, if sentimentalists seek to persuade him that the "ages of faith," the twelfth and thirteenth centuries, for instance, were better than our own, let him read any trustworthy book on the subject—[Henry Charles] Lea's "History of the Inquisition," for instance, or [George Gordon] Coulton's abridgment of Salimbene's memoirs. He will be undeceived and will be devoutly thankful that his lot has been cast in the present age, in spite of all its faults.

It would be hopeless to try to enumerate all the books I read, or even all the kinds. The foregoing is a very imperfect answer to a question which admits of only such an answer.

Notes

Full citations can be found in the selected bibliography.

1. Roosevelt, *Realizable Ideals*, 615–16.
2. Buchan, *Sidelights and Adventures*, 22.
3. *American Ideals*, 4.
4. Russell, *Life and Work*, 76.
5. Ibid., 193.
6. Ibid., 194.
7. Fulton, *Roosevelt's Writings*, xiii.
8. Wagenknecht, *Seven Worlds*, 6.
9. Ibid., 33.
10. Gleeson, *William Jennings Bryan*, 127.
11. Cole, *The Coming Terror*, 21.
12. Ibid.
13. Ibid.
14. Ibid., 23.
15. Belloc, *Biographer's Art*, 33.
16. Pallin, *Literary English and Scottish Sermons*, 101.
17. Jones, *Degenerate Moderns*, 9.
18. Roosevelt, *American Ideals*, 5.
19. Russell, *Life and Work*, 76.

PART 1: THE LIFE OF THEODORE ROOSEVELT

1. Russell, *Life and Work*, 258.
2. Roosevelt, *Progressive Principles*, 22.
3. Russell, *Life and Work*, 240.
4. Ibid.
5. Ibid.
6. Ibid.
7. Miller, *Roosevelt*, 531.
8. Roosevelt, *Autobiography*, 13.
9. Robinson, *My Brother*, 23.
10. Morris, *Rise of Roosevelt*, 60.

11. Russell, *Life and Work*, 76.

12. Roosevelt, *Autobiography*, 14.

13. Morris, *Rise of Roosevelt*, 48.

14. Russell, *Life and Work*, 29.

15. Roosevelt, *Autobiography*, 22.

16. Miller, *Roosevelt*, 64.

17. Ibid., 69.

18. Ibid.

19. Russell, *Life and Work*, 191.

20. Ibid., 192.

21. Wills, *Letters and Speeches*, 86.

22. Morris, *Rise of Roosevelt*, 50.

23. Miller, *Roosevelt*, 87.

24. Ibid., 90.

25. Miller, *Roosevelt*, 101.

26. Morris, *Rise of Roosevelt*, 136.

27. Ibid., 135.

28. Wills, *Letters and Speeches*, 200.

29. Russell, *Life and Work*, 88.

30. Wills, *Letters and Speeches*, 86.

31. Miller, *Roosevelt*, 119.

32. Ibid., 122.

33. Russell, *Life and Work*, 197.

34. Ibid., 198.

35. Miller, *Roosevelt*, 142.

36. Wills, *Letters and Speeches*, 55.

37. Miller, *Roosevelt*, 149.

38. Ibid., 109.

39. Ibid., 155.

40. Ibid.

41. Russell, *Life and Work*, 214.

42. Ibid., 116.

43. Miller, *Roosevelt*, 163–64.

44. Morris, *Rise of Roosevelt*, 298.

45. Russell, *Life and Work*, 116.

46. Wills, *Letters and Speeches*, 44.

47. Morris, *Rise of Roosevelt*, 303.

48. Ibid.

49. Ibid.
50. Miller, *Roosevelt*, 184.
51. Russell, *Life and Work*, 132.
52. Miller, *Roosevelt*, 198.
53. Russell, *Life and Work*, 134.
54. Ibid., 135.
55. Ibid., 302.
56. Ibid., 152.
57. Lowe, *Roosevelt and War*, 57.
58. Miller, *Roosevelt*, 274.
59. Lowe, *Roosevelt and War*, 235.
60. Roosevelt, *Autobiography*, 355,
61. Fulton, *Roosevelt's Writings*, 141.
62. Russell, *Life and Work*, 391.
63. Miller, *Roosevelt*, 346.
64. Ibid., 352.
65. Wills, *Letters and Speeches*, vii.
66. Fulton, *Roosevelt's Writings*, 142.
67. Miller, *Roosevelt*, 381.
68. Russell, *Life and Work*, 341.
69. Miller, *Roosevelt*, 436.
70. Russell, *Life and Work*, 360.
71. Russell, *Political Battle of 1912*, 285.
72. Ibid., 286.
73. Ibid., 289.
74. Ibid.
75. Hewlitt, *American Impact*, 184.
76. Russell, *Political Battle of 1912*, 2.
77. Wilson, *New Freedom*, 3.
78. Ibid.
79. Ibid., 7.
80. Ibid., 4.
81. Ibid.
82. Ibid., 35.
83. Ibid., 50.
84. Ibid., 14.
85. Riis, *Roosevelt the Citizen*, 201.
86. Roosevelt, *Foes of Our Own Household*, 97.

87. Riis, *Roosevelt the Citizen*, 285.

88. Russell, *Political Battle of 1912*, 204.

89. Ibid., 205.

90. Ibid., 93.

91. Hewlitt, *American Impact*, 184.

92. Russell, *Life and Work*, 261.

93. Miller, *Roosevelt*, 261.

94. Ibid., 562.

95. Ibid.

96. Russell, *Life and Work*, 341.

97. Miller, *Roosevelt*, 566.

98. Ibid.

99. Ibid.

100. Wills, *Letters and Speeches*, 277.

101. Fulton, *Roosevelt's Writings*, xx–xxi.

102. Ibid.

103. Ibid., xix.

104. Carson, *The Growth of America*, 235.

105. Dallimore, *Long Shadow*, 284.

106. Hebrews 11:4.

PART 2: THE CHARACTER OF THEODORE ROOSEVELT

1. Russell, *Life and Work*, 257.

2. Wagenknecht, *Seven Worlds*, 165.

3. Roosevelt, *Foes of Our Own Household*, 149.

4. Fulton, *Roosevelt's Writings*, 29.

5. Russell, *Life and Work*, 288.

6. Ibid., 289.

7. Ibid.

8. Roosevelt, *Realizable Ideals*, 665.

9. Roosevelt, *Autobiography*, vii.

10. Ibid., 7.

11. Riis, *Roosevelt the Citizen*, 444.

12. Ibid., 445.

13. Roosevelt, *Autobiography*, 8.

14. Ibid.

15. Riis, *Roosevelt the Citizen*, 447.

16. Ibid., 445.

17. Ibid.
18. Wills, *Letters and Speeches*, 76.
19. Goldman, *Strenuous Life*, 38.
20. Ibid., 39.
21. Ibid.
22. Fulton, *Roosevelt's Writings*, 166.
23. Goldman, *Strenuous Life*, 39.
24. Fulton, *Roosevelt's Writings*, 68.
25. Ibid., xiv.
26. Russell, *Life and Work*, 312.
27. Ibid.
28. Ibid., 209.
29. Wagenknecht, *Seven Worlds*, 38.
30. Ibid., 45.
31. Abbot, *Guide to Reading*, 120.
32. Wagenknecht, *Seven Worlds*, 76.
33. Ibid., 44.
34. Ibid.
35. Ibid., 33.
36. Ibid., 32.
37. Ibid.
38. Ibid.
39. Lever, *Roosevelt Mythos*, 204.
40. Johnson, *Theodore Roosevelt*, 73.
41. Wagenknecht, *Seven Worlds*, 8.
42. Ibid., 6.
43. Lever, *Roosevelt Mythos*, 191.
44. Ibid., 191.
45. Ibid., 192.
46. Ibid.
47. Wills, *Letters and Speeches*, 94.
48. Proverbs 29:18.
49. Wagenknecht, *Seven Worlds*, 1.
50. *Richard III*, 1.3.358.
51. Wagenknecht, *Seven Worlds*, 181.
52. Ibid.
53. Fulton, *Roosevelt's Writings*, xxvi.
54. Evans and Berent, *Quotable Conservative*, 40.

55. Roosevelt, *Foes of Our Own Household*, 47.

56. Ibid.

57. Fulton, *Roosevelt's Writings*, 155.

58. Ibid., 36.

59. Lever, *Roosevelt Mythos*, 59.

60. Roosevelt, *Race Riots, Reds, and Crime*, 101.

61. Wills, *Letters and Speeches*, 81.

62. Hewlitt, *American Impact*, 21.

63. Wills, *Letters and Speeches*, 56.

64. Ibid., 58.

65. Ibid.

66. Ibid.

67. Ibid., xli.

68. Ibid.

69. Fulton, *Roosevelt's Writings*, 200.

70. Wills, *Letters and Speeches*, 46.

71. Ibid., 2.

72. Ibid., 451.

73. Roosevelt, *Presidential Addresses and State Papers*, 1:231.

74. Wills, *Letters and Speeches*, 232.

75. Lever, *Roosevelt Mythos*, 206.

76. Hewlitt, *American Impact*, 202.

77. Lodge and Roosevelt, *Hero Tales*, xxiii.

78. Chesterton, *Omnibus*, 142–43.

79. Hewlitt, *American Impact*, 202.

80. Ibid., 203.

81. Wagenknecht, *Seven Worlds*, 151.

82. Ibid., 152.

83. Wills, *Letters and Speeches*, 288.

84. Wagenknecht, *Seven Worlds*, 155.

85. Ibid., 152.

86. Fulton, *Roosevelt's Writings*, 79.

87. Ibid.

88. Wills, *Letters and Speeches*, 202.

89. Ibid., 88.

90. Ibid., 202.

91. Ibid.

92. Ibid.

93. Johnson, *American Monarch*, 288.

94. Lowe, *Roosevelt and War*, 15.

95. Russell, *Life and Work*, 205.

96. Lowe, *Roosevelt and War*, 17

97. Wagenknecht, *Seven Worlds*, 38.

98. Ibid., 42.

99. Lever, *Roosevelt Mythos*, 43.

100. Wagenknecht, *Seven Worlds*, 42.

101. Johnson, *American Monarch*, 44.

102. Ibid.

103. Miller, *Theodore Roosevelt*, 511.

104. Lever, *Roosevelt Mythos*, 48.

105. Miller, *Roosevelt*, 37.

106. Russell, *Life and Work*, 85.

107. Wagenknecht, *Seven Worlds*, 80.

108. Fulton, *Roosevelt's Writings*, xviii.

109. Ibid., xix.

110. Lever, *Roosevelt Mythos*, 46.

111. Russell, *Life and Work*, 361.

112. Lever, *Roosevelt Mythos*, 46.

113. Ibid., 48.

114. Wills, *Letters and Speeches*, 111.

115. Wagenknecht, *Seven Worlds*, 16.

116. Fulton, *Roosevelt's Writings*, 29.

117. Lever, *Roosevelt Mythos*, vii.

118. Ibid., viii.

119. Fulton, *Roosevelt's Writings*, 168.

120. Lever, *Roosevelt Mythos*, 88.

121. Ibid.

122. Wagenknecht, *Seven Worlds*, 162.

123. Ibid.

124. Ibid.

125. Lever, *Roosevelt Mythos*, 89.

126. Johnson, *American Monarch*, 322.

127. Ibid., 323.

128. Wagenknecht, *Seven Worlds*, 114.

129. Ibid., 110.

130. Ibid., 8.

131. Lever, *Roosevelt Mythos*, 44.

132. Wagenknecht, *Seven Worlds*, 111.

133. Ibid.

134. Ibid.

135. Lever, *Roosevelt Mythos*, xiv.

136. Ibid.

137. Wagenknecht, *Seven Worlds*, 111.

138. Lever, *Roosevelt Mythos*, 191.

139. Roosevelt, *Foes of Our Own Household*, 168.

140. Johnson, *American Monarch*, 44.

141. Ibid.

142. Ibid.

143. Roosevelt, *Foes of Our Own Household*, 152.

144. Kennedy, *Birth Control in America*, 146–47.

145. Ibid.

146. Wagenknecht, *Seven Worlds*, 86.

147. Roosevelt, *Foes of Our Own Household*, 152.

148. Ibid.

149. *The Woman Rebel*, June 1914.

150. Ibid.

151. Wills, *Letters and Speeches*, 56.

152. Roosevelt, *Social Justice and Popular Rule*, 334.

153. Ibid., 335.

154. Wills, *Letters and Speeches*, 234.

155. Ibid., 23.

156. Dyer, *Theodore Roosevelt and the Idea of Race*, 105.

157. Fulton, *Roosevelt's Writings*, 165.

158. Wagenknecht, *Seven Worlds*, 186.

159. Ibid.

160. Dyer, *Roosevelt and Race*, 105.

161. Johnson, *American Monarch*, 356.

162. Ibid.

163. Ibid.

164. Russell, *Life and Work*, 261.

165. Johnson, *American Monarch*, 1.

166. Fulton, *Roosevelt's Writings*, 16.

167. Johnson, *American Monarch*, 109.

168. Lodge and Roosevelt, *Hero Tales*, xxiii.

169. Ibid.

170. Fulton, *Roosevelt's Writings*, x.

171. Ibid., xxxiv.

172. Ibid.

173. Lord Charnwood, *Theodore Roosevelt*, 47.

174. Russell, *Life and Work*, 122.

175. Ibid., 123.

176. Johnson, *American Monarch*, 274.

177. Fulton, *Roosevelt's Writings*, xxxiv.

178. Johnson, *American Monarch*, 276.

179. Roosevelt, *Foes of Our Own Household*, 130.

180. Wagenknecht, *Seven Worlds*, 182.

181. Lowe, *Roosevelt and War*, 49.

182. Roosevelt, *Foes of Our Own Household*, 132.

183. Roosevelt, *Autobiography*, 11.

184. *Trinity Hymnal*, 94.

185. Wagenknecht, *Seven Worlds*, 182.

186. Crunden, *Ministers of Reform*, 3.

187. Wills, *Letters and Speeches*, 86.

188. Ibid., 90.

189. Lever, *Roosevelt Mythos*, 191.

190. Hewlitt, *American Impact*, 174.

191. Wills, *Letters and Speeches*, 59.

192. Lever, *Roosevelt Mythos*, 191.

193. Ibid., 192.

194. Wills, *Letters and Speeches*, 254.

195. Johnson, *American Monarch*, 91.

196. Wagenknecht, *Seven Worlds*, 183.

197. Johnson, *American Monarch*, 33.

198. Ibid., 98.

199. Roosevelt, *Foes of Our Own Household*, 3.

200. Grant, *Blood of the Moon*, 105–7.

201. Johnson, *American Monarch*, 229.

202. Ibid.

203. Russell, *Life and Work*, 261.

204. Johnson, *American Monarch*, 229.

205. Crunden, *Ministers of Reform*, 3.

206. Fulton, *Roosevelt's Writings*, 73.

207. Hewlitt, *American Impact*, vi.
208. Russell, *Life and Work*, 262.
209. Lever, *Roosevelt Mythos*, 322
210. Miller, *Theodore Roosevelt*, 566.
211. Russell, *Life and Work*, 276.
212. Fulton, *Roosevelt's Writings*, 166.
213. Wagenknecht, *Seven Worlds*, 3.
214. Lever, *Roosevelt Mythos*, 2.
215. Colossians 4:5, ASV.
216. Wagenknecht, *Seven Worlds*, 4.
217. Lever, *Roosevelt Mythos*, 2.
218. Wills, *Letters and Speeches*, 36.
219. Ibid.

PART 3: THE LEGACY OF THEODORE ROOSEVELT

1. Roosevelt, *Foes of Our Own Household*, 3.
2. Ibid., 152.
3. Ibid., 132.
4. Ibid.
5. Ibid.
6. Ibid., 132–33.
7. Wills, *Letters and Speeches*, 59.
8. Ibid., 60.
9. Ibid.
10. Braxton, *Gouverneur Morris*, 101.
11. Ibid.
12. Wills, *Letters and Speeches*, 34.
13. Roosevelt, *Realizable Ideals*, 650.
14. Wills, *Letters and Speeches*, 34.
15. Ibid., 67.
16. Ibid.
17. Ibid., 68.
18. Eberstadt, *Isaac and His Devils*, 89.
19. Washington, *Programs and Papers*, 33.
20. Van Valkenburg, *Inspiration of Theodore Roosevelt*, 233.
21. Ibid., 233–34.
22. Ibid., 234.
23. Goldman, *Strenuous Life*, 39.

Selected Bibliography

BOOKS BY THEODORE ROOSEVELT

1882   *The Naval War of 1812*

1885   *Hunting Tips of a Ranchman*

1887   *Thomas Hart Benton*

1888   *Essays on Practical Politics*

        Gouverneur Morris

        Ranch Life and the Hunting Trail

1889   *The Winning of the West*, vols. 1 and 2

1891   *New York*

1893   *The Wilderness Hunter*

        American Big Game, with George Bird Grinnell

1894   *The Winning of the West*, vol. 3

1895   *Hero Tales from American History*, with Henry Cabot Lodge

        Hunting in Many Lands, with George Bird Grinnell

1897   *American Ideals*

        Some American Game

        Trail and Campfire, with George Bird Grinnell

1899   *The Rough Riders*

1900   *Oliver Cromwell*

        The Strenuous Life

1902   *The Deer Family*, with T. S. Van Dyke, D. G. Elliot, and A. J. Stone

1904   *Addresses and Messages*

1905   *Outdoor Pastimes of an American Hunter*

1907   *Good Hunting*

1909   *Outlook Editorials*

1910   *African and European Addresses*

        African Game Trails

American Problems

The New Nationalism

Presidential Addresses and State Papers, 8 vols.

1912   *The Conservation of Womanhood and Childhood*

Realizable Goals

1913   *Autobiography*

History As Literature

Progressive Principles

1914   *Through the Brazilian Wilderness*

African Game Animals, with Edmund Heller

1915   *America and the World War*

1916   *A Book-Lover's Holiday in the Open*

Fear God and Take Your Own Part

1917   *The Foes of Our Own Household*

Social Justice and Popular Rule

National Strength and International Duty

1918   *The Great Adventure*

ROOSEVELT BOOKS CITED IN THE TEXT

American Ideals. New York: Scribner's, 1901.

Autobiography. New York: Scribner's, 1924.

Foes of Our Own Household. New York: Scribner's, 1917.

Hero Tales from American History (with Henry Cabot Lodge). New York: Century, 1895.

Presidential Addresses and State Papers. 8 vols. New York: Review of Reviews, 1910.

Progressive Principles. New York: Scribner's, 1926.

Realizable Ideals. New York: Scribner's, 1919.

Social Justice and Popular Rule. New York: Scribner's, 1926.

COLLECTIONS OF THEODORE ROOSEVELT'S WRITINGS

Bishop, Joseph Bucklin, ed. *Letters to His Children*. New York: Scribner's, 1926.

Hagedorn, Hermann, ed. *The Memorial Edition of the Works of Theodore Roosevelt*. 24 vols. New York: Scribner's, 1926.

Morrison, Elting, ed. *The Letters of Theodore Roosevelt.* 2 vols. Cambridge, MA: Harvard University Press, 1951.

Wills, James Austin. *The Letters and Speeches of Theodore Roosevelt.* New York: Billington and Sons, 1937.

BOOKS ABOUT THEODORE ROOSEVELT

Lord Charnwood. *Theodore Roosevelt.* Boston: Atlantic Monthly, 1923.

Collier, Peter. *The Roosevelts: An American Saga.* New York: Simon & Schuster, 1994.

Dallimore, James. *The Long Shadow.* New York: Allan and Digby, 1962.

Dyer, Thomas. *Theodore Roosevelt and the Idea of Race.* Baton Rouge: Louisiana State University Press, 1980.

Fulton, Maurice, ed. *Roosevelt's Writings.* New York: Macmillan, 1922.

Hagedorn, Hermann. *Life of Theodore Roosevelt.* New York: Harper Brothers, 1918.

———. *The Roosevelt Family of Sagamore Hill.* New York: Macmillan, 1954.

Hewlitt, Jonathan. *The American Impact.* London: Caprice and Meadows, 1956.

Howland, Harold. *Theodore Roosevelt and His Times.* New Haven, CT: Yale University Press, 1921.

Jeffers, H. Paul. *Commissioner Roosevelt.* New York: John Wiley & Sons, 1994.

Johnson, David. *Theodore Roosevelt: American Monarch.* Philadelphia: American History Sources, 1981.

Lever, James. *The Roosevelt Mythos.* New York: Dorrit-Justin, 1923.

Lowe, Mark Hammond. *Roosevelt and War.* New York: Garamond, 1922.

Longworth, Alice Roosevelt. *Crowded Hours.* New York: Scribner's, 1933.

Miller, Nathan. *Theodore Roosevelt: A Life.* New York: William Morrow, 1992.

Morris, Charles. *The Marvelous Career of Theodore Roosevelt.* New York: John Winston, 1910.

Morris, Edmund. *The Rise of Theodore Roosevelt.* New York: Coward, McCann, and Geoghegan, 1979.

Riis, Jacob. *Theodore Roosevelt the Citizen.* New York: Macmillan, 1904.

Robinson, Corinne Roosevelt. *My Brother: Theodore Roosevelt.* New York: Scribner's, 1921.

Roosevelt, Archibald, ed. *Race, Riots, Reds, and Crime.* New York: Roosevelt Memorial Association, 1939.

Russell, Thomas, ed. *Life and Work of Theodore Roosevelt.* New York: L. H. Walter, 1919.

Thayer, William Roscoe. *Theodore Roosevelt*. New York: Houghton Mifflin, 1919.

Wagenknecht, Edward. *The Seven Worlds of Theodore Roosevelt*. New York: Longmans and Green, 1958.

Wilson, Dorothy Clarke. *Alice and Edith*. New York: Doubleday, 1989.

Wister, Owen. *Roosevelt: The Story of a Friendship*. New York: Macmillan, 1930.

OTHER BOOKS CITED

Abbot, Lyman ed. *A Guide to Reading*. New York: Doubleday, 1917.

Belloc, Hilaire. *The Biographer's Art: Excerpts from Belloc's Florid Pen*. London: Catholic Union, 1956.

Braxton, James Carter. *Gouverneur Morris*. Charleston, SC: Braden-Lowell Press, 1911.

Buchan, John. *Sidelights and Adventures*. Edinburgh, UK: Ballantine Press, 1946.

Carson, Clarence. *The Growth of America*. Greenville, AL: American Textbook Committee, 1981.

Chesterton, G. K. *Omnibus*. London: Stratford Lewes, 1966.

Cole, Harold Tribble. *The Coming Terror: Life Before the Great War*. New York: Languine Bros., 1936.

Crunden, Robert. *Ministers of Reform: The Progressives' Achievement in American Civilization, 1889–1920*. New York: Basic Books, 1982.

Eberstadt, Fernanda. *Isaac and His Devils*. New York: Viking, 1990.

Evans, Rod, and Irwin Berent, eds. *The Quotable Conservative: The Giants of Conservatism on Liberty, Freedom, Individual Responsibility, and Traditional Virtues*. Holbrook, MA: Adams, 1995.

Gleeson, Howard. *William Jennings Bryan*. New York: Ingles and Bryson, 1923.

Goldman, Horace. *The Strenuous Life*. New York: George Dial, 1958.

Grant, George. *The Blood of the Moon: The Roots of the Middle East Crisis*. Brentwood, TN: Wolgemuth & Hyatt, 1991.

Jones, E. Michael. *Degenerate Moderns: Modernity As Rationalized Sexual Misbehavior*. San Francisco: Ignatius Press, 1993.

Kennedy, David. Birth Control in America: The Career of Margaret Sanger. New Haven, CT: Yale University Press, 1970.

Pallin, Howard F., ed. *Literary English and Scottish Sermons*. London: Windus Etheridge, 1937.

Russell, Thomas. *The Political Battle of 1912*. New York: L. H. Walter, 1912.

Trinity Hymnal. Atlanta, GA: Great Commission, 1990.

Van Valkenburg, E. A. *The Inspiration of Theodore Roosevelt*. New York: Scribner's, 1924.

Washington, George. *Programs and Papers*. Washington, DC: Washington Bicentennial Committee, 1932.

Wilson, Woodrow. *The New Freedom: A Call for Emancipation of the General Energies of a People*. New York: Doubleday, Page, and Co., 1913.

Index

Printed in the USA
CPSIA information can be obtained
at www.ICGtesting.com
JSHW021354250324
59871JS00001B/31